Join Me on a Treasure Hunt:

Out and About in Florence

Ellen Reynolds

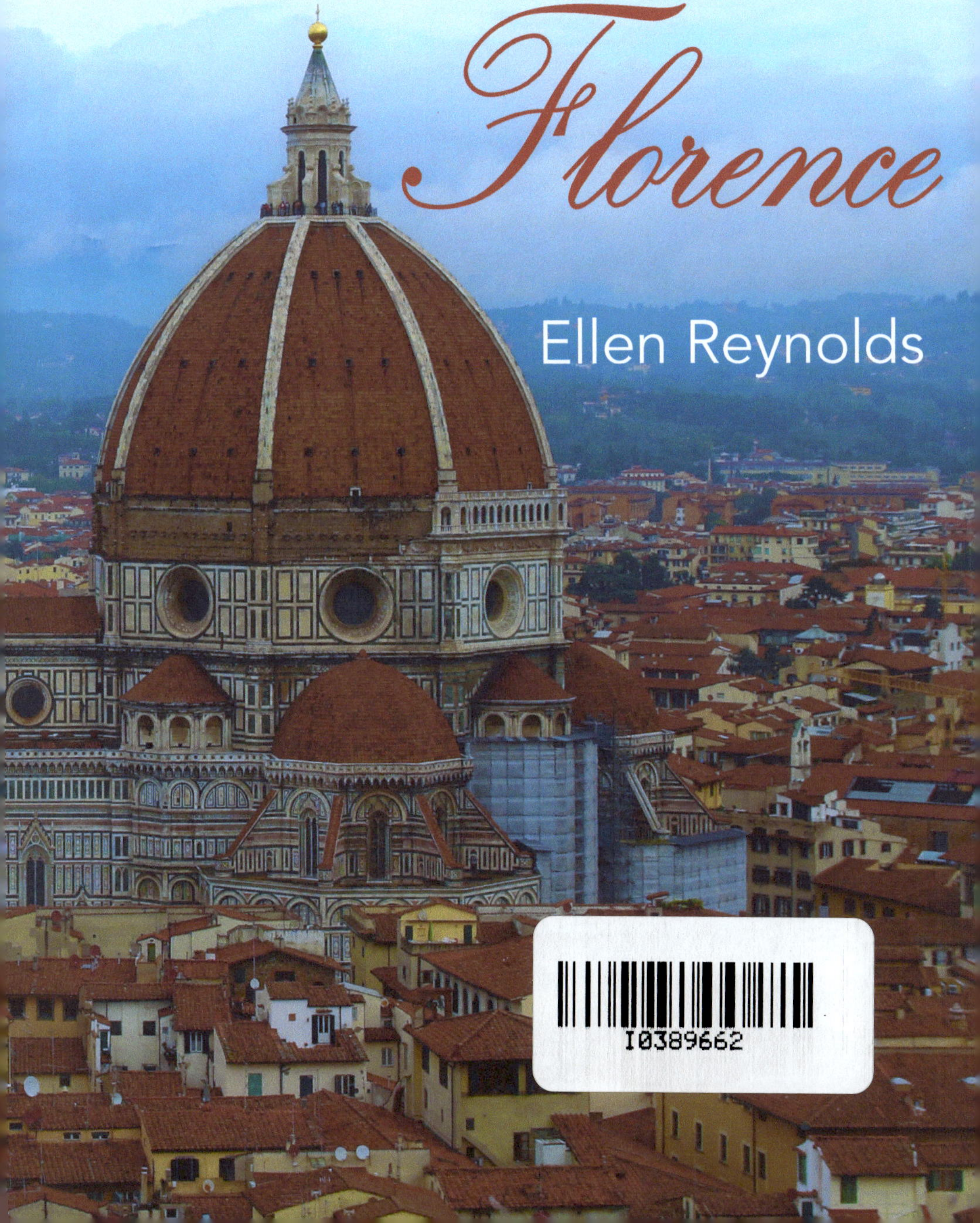

Copyright © 2021 by Ellen Reynolds

All rights reserved. No part of this book may be reproduced or transmitted in any form or by any means, electronic or mechanical, including: photocopying, recording, or by any information storage and retrieval system, without permission in writing from the copyright owner. This work is based on the experiences of an individual. Every effort has been made to ensure the accuracy of the content.

Out and About In Florence
Author: Ellen Reynolds
Editor: Marla McKenna
Associate Editor: Christa E. Reynolds
Associate Editor: Griffin Mill
Proofreader: Lyda Rose Haerle
Cover Design and Interior Layout: Michael Nicloy

All images contained in this book are owned by the author.
Florence map: www.planetware.com

Paperback ISBN-13: 978-1-945907-75-6
Ebook ISBN: 978-1-945907-82-1

PUBLISHED BY NICO 11 PUBLISHING & DESIGN,
MUKWONAGO, WISCONSIN
www.nico11publishing.com

Quantity and wholesale order requests can be emailed to:
mike@nico11publishing.com
or be made by phone: 217.779.9677

Printed in The United States of America

Dedicated to my beautiful Christa and Jamie.

Introduction

There are so very many guide books available about Florence! In this scavenger hunt, I wanted to offer something different and interactive. Years ago, when my young children and I made our first journey to Florence, I was concerned they would be overwhelmed by the sheer amount of history. So, I got out my art books (I'm an art teacher)and I went to the library—this was before the internet. I put together a Treasure Hunt of interesting items for my children to search for. They really enjoyed this challenge and also found amazing things on their own. We all had a fun introduction to the Renaissance, and were left wanting to learn and find more. This gave me the idea to write a book. I started but had many detours along the way. For two Autumns I rented a dream apartment on Borgo Allegri, the same small street the artist Cimabue lived on near Santa Croce. Wandering the streets, I felt most alive. During the day I would walk and gather information, make plans, and take photos. In the evening, I would write in my apartment or at a local restaurant. I so hope you enjoy this book as much as I did creating it for you. I want to return and continue with many more adventures!

Please, rub the Boar's nose in the Piazza del Mercato Nuovo so we may all return to this amazing place!

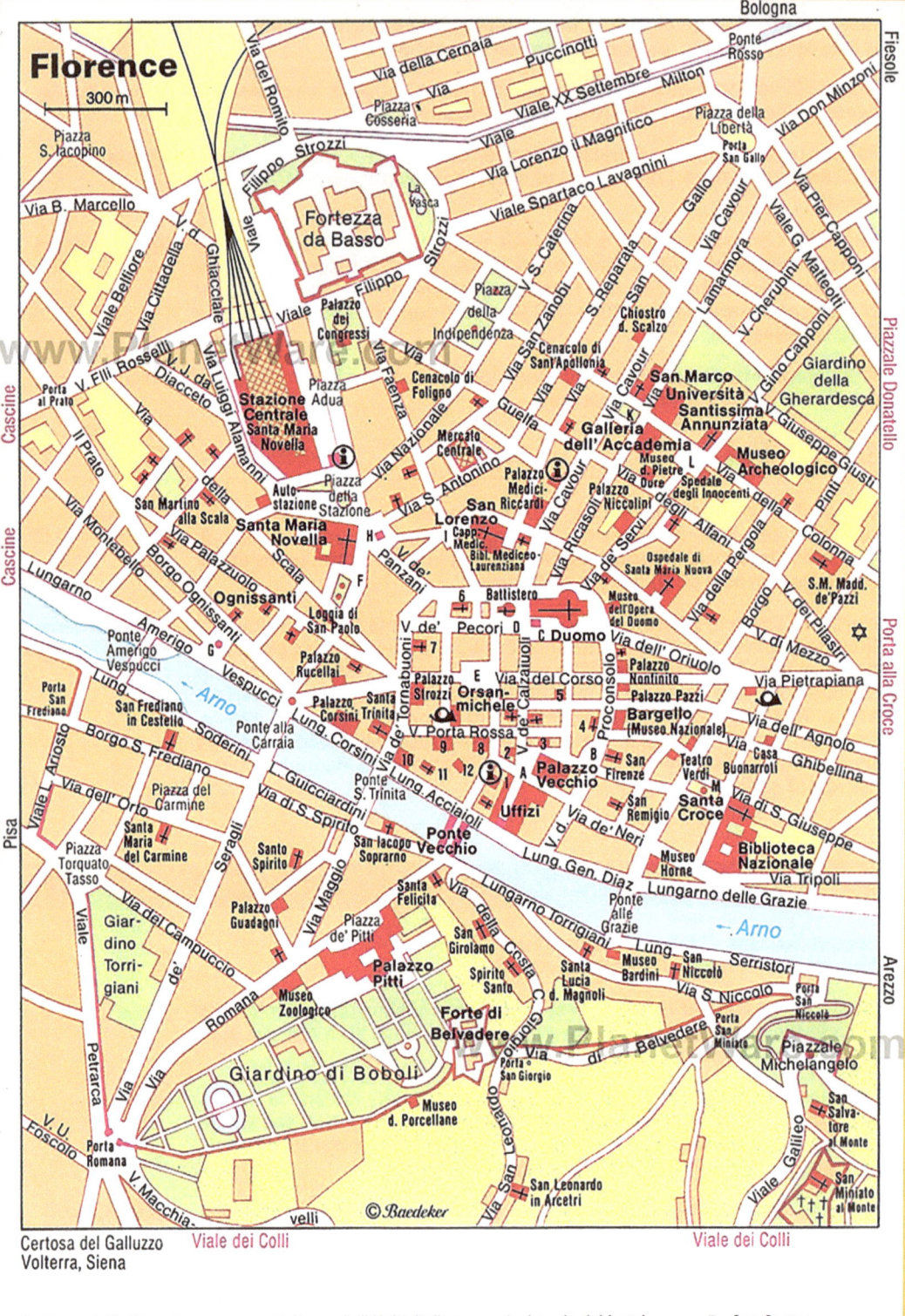

Out and About in Florence

Route One: Page 13

Route Two: Page 87

Route Three: Page 137

Things to Look For
During Your Adventure: Page 162

Glossary: Page 173

Sources: Page 181

All journeys have secret destinations of which the traveler is unaware.

Martin Buber

Route One

Greetings to you all, I hope that you are looking forward to an exciting day enjoying your first "Scavenger Hunt," which in Italian is "Caccia al Tesoro" or a hunt for treasure. You will be searching for and learning about interesting places and works of art on this journey, discovering things that are sometimes hidden and sometimes not. I will give you lots of hints, so don't worry—it won't be difficult. It will be amazing. I'll show you wondrous sites and tell you miraculous stories about real miracles. There is so much to see in this incredibly breathtaking city, everywhere you look—up, down, and all around. There is nowhere else in this world that compares to the city of Florence. So relax, put on a pair of comfortable shoes, and let's explore. The fun is in the journey and the journey is fun!

Your Guide,
Ellen

The Piazza of Santa Maria Novella

Our first adventure will take place in the Piazza Santa Maria Novella.

Don't forget your walking shoes as we will be walking quite a bit and some of the streets are uneven.

When you arrive in the piazza, which means plaza or square, have a seat on one of the benches facing the front, or what is called the façade of the Church. Let's look at some very unique designs decorating this church.

This piazza was built in1287.

The Façade

The lower portion of the façade, which is covered in green and white marble, was completed in the year 1350. At this time, brick burial vaults, or avelli, were added along the bottom and built directly into the arched niches. The upper portion of the church was designed by the architect and artist Leon Battista Alberti from 1458 to 1470. He harmonized his design with the lower section by also combining the green and white marble geometric patterns.

The six brick burial vaults, from the old façade, still remain after the expansion. This is due to their location under the supporting arches of the building. These burial vaults continue and wrap around the church's east side.

Look to the façade for a large sun, which is located in the tympanum, or the triangle shape, at the top of the Church. The sun is the emblem for this neighborhood—Santa Maria Novella.

Find the astrolabe located on the left-hand side of the façade. An astrolabe, or armillary sphere, represents the heavens, moon, and stars circling the Earth and the sun; this was placed here in 1572.

Now, let's look for a gnomon, or sundial, added in 1574. Located to the right, it is an upright marble sundial that casts its shadow onto the flat surface of the façade to tell the time and the seasons of the year.

The Sails

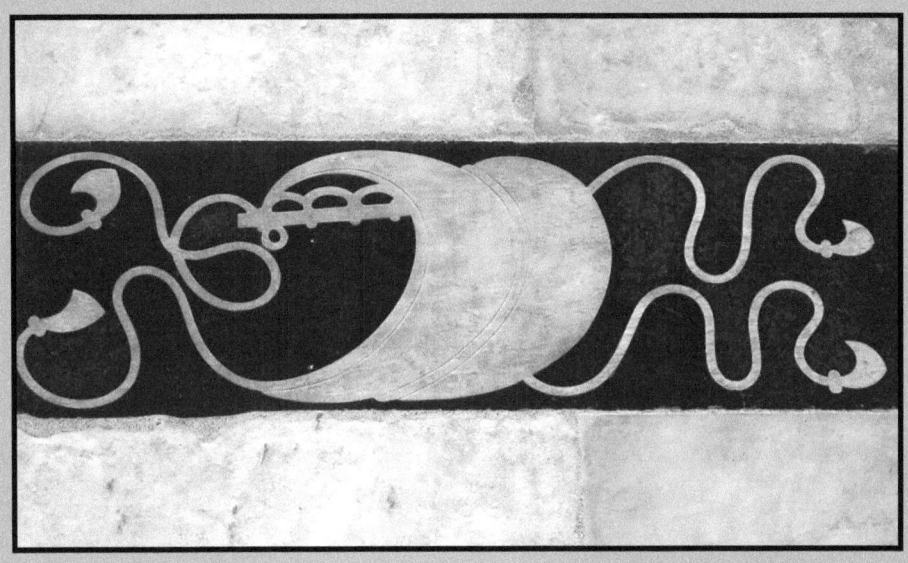

A beautiful string of sails, appearing like the windblown sails on a ship, run across the front with separate single sails on each side. This is the Rucellai family emblem called "The Sails of Fortune." The Rucellais became very rich from the dyes they developed and used in the manufacturing of fabric. Their specialty was a red dye known as "poor man's crimson." This family was the main donor, or the patrons, who contributed money for the completion of the church. The Latin writing across the top of the façade is the name of Giovanni Rucellai and the year 1470.

The volutes, or curved circular pieces, on either side of the central, round window were added in 1458 to 1470 by Alberti to hide the small roofs over the side chapels. The volute on the right was only placed here in 1920. The church's current tower stands on the base of a fallen ancient tower which was used to watch for fires. Look into the Piazza for the two large marble obelisks. An obelisk is a tall four-sided narrowing pillar with a pyramidal top.

Each is supported by four large, bronze turtles with the Florentine lily decorating their tops. Designed by the famous artist, Giambologna, they were used as turning posts for chariot races held here during the 16th century. Don't you think the turtles are really cute?

There is a small fee to enter the church if you would like to go in. I highly recommend that you do! This is an incredible introduction to early Florence.

The church of Santa Maria Novella holds much important history, of the great time of learning, named the Renaissance. You enter the church through the iron gates to the right of the façade. While standing at the gates, look to either side at the stone lambs. These are the emblem, or coat of arms, of the Wool Guild. In Florence, guilds were known as an "arti." I used to think they were religious symbols, but they are not. You will notice this emblem throughout the city because the Wool Guild was extremely powerful and very wealthy. They were called the Arti di Calimala. Formed in 1182, they were the wool merchants and cloth finishers who sold merchandise throughout Europe. This helped them become wealthy, and they were the main contributors to most city projects. Search for the lambs; they are everywhere in the city.

 The courtyard you enter is actually an old cemetery which holds burial markers along the walls and ground. This is called the Via degli Avelli cemetery, named after the church's burial vaults which are located in the façade.

 This cemetery was enlarged in 1219 and then again in 1245. Follow along the pathway to the ticket booth, and then enter the church thru the side doors located in front of you. When you are inside, walk to the left toward the huge front doors, and turn to the main altar facing the end of the aisle.

 Let me tell you some history about the church. In the year 983, Santa Maria Vigne Church was the original building which stood here. The church was very small and located outside the city walls in the vineyards or Vigne. This entire area was abandoned during a horrible plague and was rebuilt in 1090 and then again in 1279.

During this time a Dominican Friar held sermons which were so popular that all of the people were unable to fit inside the church. So, they decided to build a new church, and on October 18, 1297, construction began. The first stone was laid in what is now the Gondi Chapel. The Piazza was enlarged again in 1244 and then also in 1287.

The wealthy Rucellai family became the main donors during the new rebuilding. They have a large side chapel which includes the family burial area.

During this time, wealthy citizens were expected to donate to the church.

Now, let's look toward the main altar in front of you. Can you see how the aisle, or nave, appears wider near the entrance and narrows towards the altar?

This brings your eyes forward and was done by purposely placing the pillars in an irregular line.

Look up to the vaults (the arched supports) of the ceiling and you will see the colors of black and white which represent the Dominicans. The Dominicans are an order in the Catholic religion.

The very, very, large, hanging crucifix located in the center of the aisle was designed by Giotto di Bondone between 1289 and 1312. It was completed almost 100 years before the start of the Renaissance. Giotto lived from 1267-1337 and is one of the most famous early Florentine artists and architects. It is often felt that Giotto's work was the strongest influence that contributed to the beginning of the Renaissance. The European Renaissance was one of the most important time periods in Western history, and it began in Florence in 1450 and went until 1650. The term "Renaissance" means rebirth or renewal in French. This incredible time of learning and human achievement in all forms led us out of the Dark Ages and into the Modern Ages. Giotto's crucifix is a very important piece because it is the first work of art portraying Christ as a dying man. Often this crucifix is referred to as "True Man" because it depicts Christ's body realistically hanging from the weight of itself with his blood showing from his wounds.

Now walk to your left to the third bay. Here is another important work from the early Renaissance: Masaccio's fresco of the Trinity painted in 1427. A fresco is a painting in which fresh paint pigments are applied directly into wet plaster on the wall. Masaccio, nicknamed "Moso" for "clumsy," lived a brief life from 1401-1428. Masaccio was a great follower of Giotto.

The Trinity is painted on a flat surface using the new artistic style of perspective, giving it the appearance of depth. This work is one of the first to incorporate this technique, which was taught to Masaccio by the artist Filippo Brunelleschi. Notice how the vaulted ceiling appears round, not flat, and how God and Christ seem to be retreating?

Another important detail in this painting is that the Virgin is portrayed as a woman, not as a young girl. The dove flying above represents the Holy Spirit and the two figures pictured in the foreground are of the donors.

Beneath the painting of the Trinity is a painting of a skeleton, who is giving us a strong warning! He is telling us:

"I was once what you are still and what I am you are still to be."

How true and thought provoking!

Giorgio Vasari painted over both of these works during his huge remodeling project in 1567. Luckily, the Trinity fresco was found in 1860, but the painting of the skeleton was not uncovered until 1952, almost 300 years later. The marble pulpit on the column behind the Trinity was designed by Filippo Brunelleschi in 1443; he is one of Florence's most important men. We will be learning very much about this man during our journey.

In 1565, Cosimo I commissioned the architect, painter, and biographer Giorgio Vasari to restructure this church and many other buildings in Florence for his son's upcoming marriage. Medieval altars, chapels, and frescos were removed and replaced with gray sandstone. He then added the large paintings done by numerous artists, including many done by himself. Important frescos were removed. Some saved portions can be seen in the church museum.

Follow along the wall to the Sagristia (now a bookstore) which is located higher up at the level of the old church from the 1380s.

Inside there is an incredibly ornate vaulted ceiling, and also a large wash basin by the terra cotta artist Giovanni della Robbia from 1449.

Outside the Sagristia doors are some fresco remnants left from 1335 that are underneath the clock. You are able to read about this clock on the nearby plaque—it's very interesting.

While touring, walk over to the Gondi Chapel, this is one of the most ancient areas of the church where the building's first stone was laid on October 18, 1279. The chapel also contains a crucifix created by Brunelleschi in 1410.

Near the seating area close to the main altar is a small holy water font, or stoup, standing in the corner.

The support that appears to look like a woman is called a caryatid. This water font was carved by a young Michelangelo using green marble from Egypt.

The Strozzi Chapel is located on the end of the left transept at a higher level. A transept is the aisle which crosses the main aisle forming the shape of a cross. This chapel contains frescos painted from the 1350s showing the life of Saint Thomas. Some were inspired by the great Florentine author, Dante Alighieri, who is included in the painting. He is wearing red and is to the left of the Strozzi family.

There is also a beautiful altar by Orcagna which was created between 1354 to 1357.

Now you have reached the main chapel, or Cappela Maggiore, an area that was hit by lightning in 1357. The altar from 1860, contains an urn holding the remains of Saint John of Salerno, the founder of the 1243 church. Behind the main altar are frescos done by Ghirlando and his brothers in 1485, which tell the story of Saint John the Baptist. Saint John, or San Giovanni, is the patron saint of the city of Florence. When this was painted, Michelangelo was an apprentice in Ghirlando's studio and he is thought to have helped with the frescos. These also depict scenes of life in Florence from 1486 to 1490.

Located in the rear to the right is a very large wooden lectern, or badalone. This was used to hold the choir's books. The inlaid wooden stalls along the sides are for the choir to sit upon.

To the right of the main altar is another Strozzi Chapel which holds the tomb of Filippo Strozzi. These frescos were done by the artist Filippino Lippi in 1502, who also designed the large stained glass window. Pictured on the vaulted ceiling are Adam, Noah, Jacob, and Abraham, who were important figures from the Old Testament.

The religious subjects are of Saint John and Saint Philip slaying a dragon using images from the artist's imagination. The dragon is meant to be the devil. The two soldiers painted on the right are F. Strozzi and his son, Lorenzo.

The figures appear to be jumping off the wall as he used the art of perspective in his design. **The Decameron**, a very important piece of Italian literature written by Giovanni Boccaccio in about

1348, begins in this very chapel. The story tells of a group of friends who meet on this very spot and devise  a plan to escape the devastating plague of 1348, which is thought to have taken the lives of half the population of Florence.

As you walk to the side, up the stairs, you will see the Rucellai Chapel and the family's burial area. The sarcophagus of Rucellai, the main donor, is located in the floor at the base of the stairs. He is shown draped in flowing fabric representing his profitable cloth-dyeing business.

A miracle happened in the last chapel on the right! In 1472, young boys were playing in the church, and one of them thought he heard someone calling out his name. In the chapel, you will find an image of the Virgin painted on the inside of one of the Avelli arches. She asked the boy to clean her off. So, this became the Chapel of the Madonna of Purity or della Pura. Do you think the boy helped her or was he too afraid?

When you are finished in the church, please exit through the doors opposite of where you entered, and walk out into the Great Cloister complex.

The Cloister Complex

A cloister is an open space surrounded by covered arched walkways and open on the inside, forming a square, usually attached to a church. This cloister contains 56 bays.

You will enter the Green Cloister, or the Chiostro Verde, which has paintings by Paolo Uccello depicting the flood and the life of Noah. These paintings were completed in 1397.

This cloister is named the Green Cloister because it is decorated with the terra verde style of painting, which is done using green clay. This became a popular technique because it looks like bronze.

Next, we will walk into the beautiful first cloister on the right, which is called the Cloister of the

Dead, or the Chiostrino Dei Morte. It was actually a large underground cemetery that was left below the church  when it was rebuilt in 1279. This large, ancient cloister has beautifully painted ribs spanning across the ceiling as stars are displayed on a dark blue background.

This cloister had to be rebuilt in 1337 after the flood of 1333, and it was rebuilt again after the flood of 1966. Strangely enough, both of these floods happened on November 4.

The next cloister, the Spanish Chapel, or the Cappilone degli Spagnoli, was built in 1343. It was later used by Eleanor of Toledo, Duke Cosimo I's Spanish wife.

This chapel is filled with colorful well-preserved frescos telling the story of the Passion and Resurrection. You view the cycle from left to right. In the main crowd scene are representations of many famous Florentines. Can you see Dante? He is wearing a Priori's crimson gown and cap. He is the author of **The Divine Comedy**. Dante is often thought to be the father of modern Italian

language, because he chose to write his book in Italian and most authors at the time wrote in Latin. Notice how much action is happening here; it is quite a violent picture. Look at the dogs nipping at people's heels.

These dogs represent the Dominicans, who wore black and white habits. The Dominicanes, or Hounds of the Lord, were a very busy religious group hounding out heretics for their Inquisitions.

The punished people are all around above, with a very scary painting of hell, meant to put the fear of God into all Florentines.

Outside the chapel is the Refectory, located between the Green Cloister and the Great Cloister. The Refectory is now an interesting museum housing many reliquaries and clerical garments.

Reliquaries are decorative vessels usually made of glass or crystal to hold remnants of saints. You are able to see these pieces inside the containers—very interesting. Wander around a bit if you like. We are all done! I really hope you enjoyed this ancient Church and learned some things you may not have known otherwise.

A very famous pharmacy—the Pharmacy of Santa Maria Novella—is part of the church located next door at the end of the piazza. This is a beautiful shop which carries ancient secret recipes for perfumes and luxurious soaps. They will even mix your own fragrance for you.

Now, let's walk back out to the center of the

piazza. Stand with the church façade behind you. Look to your left, and walk across the piazza to the street named Via de Banchi, this same street will soon become the Via dei Cerretani. Don't worry we won't be lost. Just keep walking straight ahead and stay on the

Via dei Cerretani which will lead you directly to the Baptistery in Piazza San Giovanni. Soon, the huge red roof of the Duomo will appear directly in front of you. Its size is staggering!

Piazza San Giovanni

The first open space you will come to is the Piazza of San Giovanni which holds the Baptistery of San Giovanni in its center. Two piazzas, Piazza San Giovanni and the Piazza de Duomo join together here to form a large open area containing many of the most important buildings and works of the Renaissance.

The Renaissance, or the Rebirth, is the historical era which followed the dark Middle Ages. It started in Florence between the 14th and 17th centuries.

First, let's take a walk around the famous Baptistery and familiarize ourselves with its façade. It is decorated using a green and white marble geometric pattern. This ancient and very important building has influenced the designs of many other buildings in Florence.

The Baptistery is one of the oldest buildings in Florence, built from 800 to 1000.

It stands upon the 5th century ruins of the Roman Temple of Mars, the Roman God of War. In Roman times, Mars was the Portafuna, or patron of the city. The city was founded by Roman veterans of war near where the Ponte Vecchio bridge is now located. Today Florence's patron saint is Saint John the Baptist, or San Giovanni in Italian.

The Baptistery

The Baptistery is constructed in an octagon shape with a pyramidal top. An octagon is used to

represent the symbol of the eighth day, or the Octavadies, which is known as the day of the Risen Christ. The current Baptistery was located in front of the church, Santa Reparta, where the Duomo now stands. In the 11th century, it was enlarged and covered with marble and stone scavenged from other ancient buildings. In the 12th century, the golden Byzantine-style interior dome was installed. Between the 14th and 16th century, its grand doors were added. Each year communal baptisms were held for all children born during that year; it was also used for a population count. White and black beans counted represented boys or girls. Many marriages and other ceremonies were also held here. Dante himself was baptized here in 1265. He called the building "My beautiful San Giovanni" in his famous writing **The Divine Comedy**. During this time, the entire Baptistery building was surrounded by cemeteries. How different from now!

Let's look along the façade for a portion of stone scavenged from a Roman sarcophagus embedded in the southwest corner. A sarcophagus is a coffin usually Greek or Roman, and the carvings in this one depicts a naval scene. These photos are shown on previous pages.

Now we will look for the two Pisian columns which are on either side of the East Baptistery doors—the gilded doors facing the Duomo. These columns have an interesting story. In 1117, the reddish-colored porphyry columns were placed between the Baptistery and the church of Santa Reparta.

Porphyry means rock containing large crystals. These were a gift to the Florentines from the city of Pisa. It is thought that the columns were originally very shiny, and they were said to contain the power of reflecting the guilt of any person who had unpunished crimes. Before gifting the columns, the Pisians smoked the shiny columns so they were unable to reflect anything at all. This was the last gift to Florence from Pisa.

Now, you are so very fortunate to be standing in front of the most exquisite doors in the world. The East Doors are also famously named "The Gates of Paradise."

This nickname is attributed to Michelangelo, who said the doors were so beautiful they were suitable to be used to enter heaven.

The East Doors were created by Lorenzo Ghiberti after winning a competition commissioned by the Wool Guild, or the Calimala. He started work on

these gold-gilded bronze doors in 1425 and did not finish until 1452. To gild means to cover with gold. There are 10 panels, and each represents an important scene from the Old Testament.

Admire how Ghiberti created the illusion of depth in each panel by using a foreground, mid-ground, and a flattened background to make the scenes appear realistic. Find the busts of Lorenzo and his son Vittorio along the doors' edges, and look at all the beautiful flora and fauna on the surroundings.

The East Doors had to go through extensive restoration after the flood of 1966, and work was only completed in 2014—48 years of hard work.

The original East Doors are now housed in the Opera di Santa Maria del Fiore Museum which is just around the corner near the Duomo. I recommend going if you have the time. Ghiberti had previously won another competition for the North Doors completed between 1403 and 1424, which also show scenes from the Old Testament and the life of Christ.

These doors, sometimes called Ports Alla Croce, include another self-portrait of Ghiberti wearing a turban. The flora and fauna on the surrounding

areas were done by the artist Uccello who loved animals, especially birds.

The first doors on the South were designed and cast in the 1330s by Andrea Pisano and show 28 quatrefoil-shaped scenes of the life of Saint John the Baptist.

Now, let me tell you a wonderful story of a miracle.

Near the entry on the north side of the Baptistery located in the piazza is a strange column standing alone, decorated with a tree. This column remembers Saint Zenobius, the first bishop of Florence in 398, who was very beloved. He died in 429. During the 9th century, it was decided his sacred body would be moved from its original burial place to the church of Santa Reparta, where the Duomo stands now. Legend says that while his coffin was being moved in the cold December winter, it brushed up against a barren elm tree that stood on this very spot. The elm tree immediately burst into full leaf after his coffin touched the tree!

    This column honors Saint Zenobius and the miracle of the flowering tree.

The original column was placed here in 430 but was washed away during the flood of 1333 and replaced with this column in 1384. Every year on May 25th is his day of celebration.

If you would like to enter the Baptistery, you will need to purchase a ticket. The single ticket will allow you access to the Baptistery, the Bell Tower or Campanile, the Opera de Duomo (which is the museum of the Duomo), the Cupola of the Duomo (the very top of the dome) and the ruins of Santa Reparta and Roman Ruins. These ruins are in the lower level of the Cathedral.

Entrance into the main cathedral is free. The ticket office is located across the street opposite the main entrance to the Baptistery at #7 Via de

Cerretani. All locations on the ticket do not need to be seen in a single day.

Golden Mosaic Tiles

The Baptistery's interior is a breathtaking surprise, with golden glass mosaics covering the entire domed ceiling.

Created in the Byzantine style of art which was used during the 13th century, these mosaics tell the stories of Genesis, Joseph, the Life of Christ, and the Last Judgement—which also portrays yet another terrifying hell!

During this time period, most people in Florence were unable to read, so the churches were covered with visual religious stories. People could "read" or interpret the meaning by looking at the stories in the pictures and carvings.

The columns inside the building are also marble and stone pillaged from ancient buildings. The amazing mosaic tile floor has a strong Arabic influence resembling a carpet.

The upper windows and arches also have Arabic and Egyptian patterns painted on them.

There is a very large Zodiac mosaic laid in the floor behind the East Doors inscribed with this message: "I am the Sun. I am the Wheel turned by fire whose turning turns the Sphere." Written in Latin, it is a palindrome which means it is a phrase that is the same forwards or backwards.

Sunlight streams down through the oculus, or the opening in the center of the dome, and onto the floor. Although this could always be used to tell the time of year, it was mostly for finding the correct date of Easter.

A metal portion in the oculus has been removed and the dial is no longer in use. If you look directly under the oculus, you can see the outline of the old baptismal font located in the floor.

This outline is square, but I have also read it used to be much larger and shaped like a rectangle.

Near the altar, there are glass panels in the floor for viewing the ruins and mosaics of older buildings.

I'm told there are portions of tile from an old Roman bakery in here, but I have looked and asked and haven't found them. Can you? When you are done looking around in this marvelous building, please exit through the South Door.

After exiting, walk just a few steps to your left. Standing with your back to the Baptistery, face the open arched building in front of you. This is the Loggia de Bigallo; a loggia is an arched terrace open on one or both sides. The Bigallo was built in 1325 for the group of the Misericordia, or the Brotherhood of Mercys. The Misericordia's purpose was to help the sick and victims of misfortune. During times of plagues, the Brothers removed cadavers from the streets while wearing black habits and covering their faces to be unknown. This group is still active in the city, and they are located across the street where the ambulances are.

St. Mary of the Bigallo's mission was to help all children.

During the 1300s, lost and abandoned children would be publicly displayed at the Bigallo for three days to see if they were found or adopted.

Look above at the two frescos painted in the arches of the loggia. One is of St. Peter, and the other is yet another strange story of a miracle.

Look at this fresco and you'll see a black horse running above a crowd of people. The story says the saint, a Dominican friar at the time, chased out the black horse, which was actually the Devil.

The friar stood in front of the devil horse and held his arms in the shape of a cross. The horse, who had been running wild through the crowd, saw the sign of the cross, and suddenly disappeared. Poof...he vanished—just gone. Another miracle!

This miracle took place at the corner of Via Strozzi and Via Vercchetti. The artist Giambologna created a little bronze Dia Volino, a devil, to commemorate the incident. The statue is there still; look upwards to find it. Now the Bigallo offers free visitor and tourist information. It also houses a small, three-room, free museum which holds many precious works of art.

Cathedral Santa Maria del Fiore

The Duomo is not called the Duomo because of its dome. Duomo means Domas Dei, or House of God, in Latin. Many churches without domes in Italy are also called Duomo. The Neo-Gothic façade was done between 1857 and 1889, with this design chosen after three worldwide competitions. The color scheme of red, white, and green marble is meant to represent the Italian flag.

Santa Reparta was the original church that stood where the Duomo is now; actually, it stood inside the Duomo. Santa Reparta was built over Roman ruins, destroyed in the 6th century and then rebuilt. As Florence's population and importance grew, a new Cathedral was needed.

On September 8, 1296, work began on Santa Maria del Fiore, or the Duomo. Its huge red tiled dome was not added until 1436. This was because no one was able to figure out how to place a dome that was the width of the walls without it all collapsing. So, the building stood roofless with the church of Santa Reparta set inside and still used for services. There were many crazy ideas about how to build the dome, but none could ever be done. Another fierce competition was held by the city guilds, and Filippo Brunelleschi won with his design.

He had devised an amazing architectural plan without the use of scaffolding. The dome he designed is actually two domes, with the inner dome used to lighten the weight load of the outer dome.

The brick of the dome is laid in a self-supporting herringbone pattern upon an octagonal base similar to the Baptistery. There are eight supporting white ribs and eight side windows. The dome stands at an amazing 384 feet tall. The dome was completed in 1436, and

only took 16 years of work. It is still one of the largest domes in the world.

The stairs to the cupola and lantern weave inside the space between the two domes. You can climb the 463 steps leading up to the top and be rewarded with a full circle view of the city and countryside. If you are afraid of heights or narrow stairways, this might not be the journey for you.

Michelozzo topped the dome with a lantern, and 25 years later, he added the gilded bronze ball and cross. It's told that the Florentines thought they were tempting God by getting too close to heaven as the Duomo continued to be made taller through these additions.

Before entering the church, walk along the façade, and let's search for a few things. If you can't find them all, it's okay. I'm sure there are many *things I have not found.*

On the right set of doors entering the façade of the church is a circle of very expressive angels; their faces are full of emotion.

Look above to the mosaic niches to the sides of the doors, and you will see statues of Santa Reparta, the saint from the original church, as well as Saint Zenobius. The metal doors are decorated with scenes of Egypt, butterflies, and salamanders.

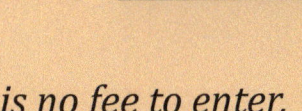

Look for a man with a snake around his neck.

There is no fee to enter.

Let's look at the main cathedral's interior. Enter through the set of front doors on the right. The interior is huge, and it can hold up to 30,000 people. Notice how plain the interior is compared to the exterior. This is why it is

sometimes called the inside-out church. Swirling inlaid marble floors contain the letters OPA which stands for the Opera of the Cathedral Works, which in Latin is "ORA pro animis" ("Pray for Souls").

Turn now, and look above the doors. High up on the wall is a very strange clock designed by Paolo Uccello in 1443. This is a 24-hour clock with 24 daisy petals showing the numbers for each hour of the day and night. Having only one hand, it runs counterclockwise like the Sun from east to west.

Another work you will see by Uccello is the green fresco of the Knight Sir John Hawkeswood, who was a mercenary in Florence for 20 years. He was promised a monument for his service, but only received a painted fresco.

Near Hawkeswood, high on the wall, there is a small painting of Dante done by Michellino in 1465. This painting shows Dante holding his book, **The Divine Comedy**, with the city of Florence shown to his right and the Circles of Hell from his book, **The Inferno**, behind him.

The choir's enclosure is built before the high

altar and the Bishop's chair sits behind. This Cathedral is the Roman Catholic Archdiocese of Florence, so the Bishop would often attend services. On the left side, behind the altar, are sets of doors with terra cotta lunettes above them, done by della Robbia. Located directly behind the altar at the very end of the church is the Altar of Saint Zenobius.

The eight-sided, eight-ribbed, eight-windowed building follows the symbolism of the Baptistery. The inside of the dome was painted by Vasari and Zuccari between 1572 and 1579. This dome has the same theme as the

Baptistery's dome: The Last Judgement. We see a scary hell where people are chewed up and spit out—the picture is meant to terrify you into being good. Looking up, you can see a viewing area that can be walked during your climb to the top of the dome, or cupeta, for an extremely close-up view.

If you purchased a ticket, you may go downstairs to view the ruins of the old church, Santa Reparta,

and also the ruins from the Roman town it was built upon. Take your time walking along the raised, lit walkways that wind you through the old mosaics and building remnants. See if you can find a tomb with a carved shield that has hedgehogs on it!

Near the gift shop, which of course you may enter without a ticket, there is a grated door. Look inside. There is Brunelleschi's tomb—the architect of the Dome. His epitaph reads, "Here lies Filippo Brunelleschi, a Florentine of Great Genius." He was able to be buried within his greatest work!

To go back outside, you will exit the carved wooden doors nearest the Bell Tower, or Campanile. The tower was designed by the city architect Giotto, who was also one of the greatest Renaissance painters and influencers. Work on this structure started in 1334 and finished in 1359, 22 years after Giotto's death and long before completion of the church. The tower is only 20 feet shorter than the dome.

Rows of carvings circling the tower show images

from the book of Genesis. There is also a row of medallions with non-religious themes depicting education, art, music, mythology, and more.

Can you find the scene from mythology?

The mythology medallion depicts the Greek inventor Daedalus flying and trying out his new wings.

Near the Campanile is a water marker, or Arno Marker, high on the Duomo wall.

These markers are placed throughout the city marking the various flood levels and dates the floods occurred.

Keep your eyes open and UP to find them everywhere. If you can find one, try to imagine the water raising to that height. Under the marker, near the small fenced-in area are names of people who were buried in the old cemetery that was between the Baptistery and the Duomo. With your ticket you can climb the bell tower; it is 414 steps to the top giving you a beautiful view of the Duomo from above.

There are stopping points, near the huge bells, along the way to rest.

Now, let's walk toward the rear of the Duomo, to enter the Piazza Duomo. Stop for a while to admire the church with all its intricate, crazy geometric patterns covering every available area.

While walking in

the Piazza Duomo, you will see on your right two very large statues. One is Arnolfo di Cambio, who was the first architect of the cathedral, and the other is Brunelleschi, who is staring up at his incredible dome.

Keep walking forward, and we'll take a short

detour onto the street to your right, the Via della Studio. This is the workshop where sculptors now make replacement reproductions for the cathedral using the old methods. You can peek inside and maybe see them at work.

Here are a few things for you to search for near the rear of the church.

On the rear wall of the church is a large head of a dog that's protruding out. It is interesting that he is there. Could he be a Dominicane howling at Santa Maria Novella? There are grotesques, which are carved

fantastical beasts, that ring all the building's sides.

Also, look down for a large round white marble disk embedded into the piazza. This disk marks the very spot where the ball and cross from the top of the lantern fell on February 16, 1660, after being hit by lightning. This was so very loud it could be heard throughout the city. Two years later it was replaced with a larger ball and cross that carry two lead containers holding holy relics for protection.

Look up to the bottom edge between the dome and church walls, and you will notice how only one portion has a carved white edge along the bottom. This will become extremely obvious once you find it.

I had never noticed it before, but now I always see it. It's said the artist working on the project asked Michelangelo for an opinion of his work. After some thought, Michelangelo replied that he thought it looked like a cricket cage which made the artist so upset he left and never completed his work.

Continue walking around to the north side of the church. Look around the corner, very high up, and try to find a hidden statue of the head of a bull. Many stories revolve about this; one story suggests that the bull statue was placed there to honor all beasts of burden that helped with the construction of the church.

Also, farther down along this side of the building are two very strange lions guarding an entrance door. There are also differing stories regarding the lions.

The line forms at the far door to climb to the Cupola though the center of the dome which is included in your ticket.

Our scavenger hunt continues onto one more extremely important place.

Come along if you'd like to join me on this journey, or you can save this adventure for another day. I'm sure you are tired. But this last stop is

definitely one of the most important sites to be seen in Florence!

If you do decide to continue with our Caccia al Tesoro, please return to the rear of the Duomo, and stand with your back toward the church. You can also start at this spot another day. Look toward your right, and walk down the street Via Dei Proconsollo toward the Bargello—the building with the tall brick tower. The Bargello used to be the city prison but now holds an incredible sculpture museum. This is an absolutely wonderful place to visit if you have time later. When you arrive at the Bargello, turn left onto the Borgo de Greci and follow it straight into the Piazza Santa Croce.

Basilica Santa Croce

Santa Croce means Holy Cross. In this large piazza, the first games of football were played. This game called Calico Storico Florentino, or Couchostorico, is fairly violent and has four

teams of 27 players representing different sections of the city. The 50-minute-long game is still played in this piazza once a year.

Hunt along the walls for the round stone marker on the side of a building to your right while facing the church.

This marker from 1565 shows the halfway point of the football playing field. Directly across is a much smaller marker, very high up, and fairly hard to find.

This piazza has many water markers, called Arno Markers, usually placed on corners. These show the water level of floods in 1333, 1466, 1547, 1844, and 1966.

Most are from the severe flood of November 4, 1966. It's exciting to find a marker from 1333; these markers are made of stone, showing waves.

This area of the city is low and swampy and is hit hardest during the floods. Imagine the water filling the city this high.

    The huge statue on the stairs of the Church of Santa Croce is of the poet Dante Alighieri. The lion, or "Marzocco," is displaying a shield with the fleur di lys; all symbols of Florence. Dante's statue was in the center of the piazza but after the flood of 1966, he was relocated here. Look at the carved shields around his base. Can you find a lady standing on an elephant? Which emblem is your favorite? Mine is the tree.

The front, or façade, of Santa Croce church was completed much later than the rest of the building, in 1863 by Niccolo Matas. His name and date are written on the upper right of the tympanum or triangle. The façade was designed to match other Florentine churches with marble imported from Egypt.

Look for the Star of David on the tympanum; this symbol represents the joining of the Old and New Testaments.

There is a small fee to enter the church. The ticket office is to the rear of the Dante statue. Search for the Arno Marker from 1557 in the aisle.

The Franciscans, followers of St. Francis, started a church here in 1220. This is still the largest Franciscan church in the world.

This was a marshy area outside the city walls where the poor workers and peasants lived. In 1252, the building became too small and a new church began. In 1280, crowds to hear the sermons grew too large for this church and it was enlarged (the same happened at Santa Maria Novella). Inquisitions were held here from 1284 to 1782. Scary!

Around 1280, the famous crucifix, created by the artist Cimabue, was installed. This large wooden crucifix is one of the first pieces that was not created in the Byzantine style of art which was used during medieval times. Cimabue is considered to be the father of Italian painting and was Giotto's teacher.

The crucifix was badly damaged in the flood of 1966 when the water height reached five meters, or 16 feet, high inside the church. This water was also mixed with oil, mud, and garbage. How horrible! It is thought this was the most important work lost during the flood. The original crucifix, partially restored, is now held in the museum of the church.

The architect, Arnolfo di Cambio was hired to enlarge the church again in 1294; during this time he was also working on the great Cathedral and the Palazzo della Signoria. He was extremely busy. Di Cambio died in 1302 having only completed the apse and the transept of the church. The apse is the curved rear of the building and Nave is the main aisle of the church. The transept crosses the Nave, and together, they form the shape of a cross. The old church located toward the front, inside the unfinished new building, was still used for services until 1320. There was a long building stoppage due to the plague, and work was not done for many years.

Santa Croce was finally finished in 1442, but the front was plain stone until 1863.

The church is also a pantheon or a building where famous dead are buried and honored, and many well-known Florentines throughout time are resting here. At least 15,000 people are buried here.

There are many guiding signs inside the church which contain much information.

Inside, the floor is covered with 270 tombe terragne, which are graves set into the earth or floor.

Many died in the 14th and 15th centuries. The oldest graves are near the altar, and most were victims of plague.

Older graves show images of the person—Knights with their sword and shield at their side, and some having a pillow beneath their head.

Try to find the sad, beautiful grave of a couple lying together in death.

Have a seat, and look up to the painted ceiling. This is a painted, wooden-trussed ceiling supported by the two rows of stone columns. The large stained glass rose window was made in 1448 and is one of the largest rose windows in the world. Rose windows are the circular stained glass windows found in many churches. It tells the story of the deposition of Christ.

Along the left wall from the entrance to your right, is the Bardi de Vernio chapel housing the sculptor Donatello's beautiful wooden crucifix.

This chapel, built for the Alberti family, has tall colorful stained glass windows designed by Agnolo Gaddi a follower of Giotto. He also designed the frescos telling the story of the cross.

The altar screen made by many 14th century artists has a predella, or platform, along its bottom telling the story of a knight.

To the right is another Bardi Chapel painted with

frescos by Giotto, done in 1320 to 1325, showing the life of St. Francis in six episodes. These are in excellent condition. They were uncovered in 1850 and were later restored.

Giotto also painted the frescos in the Peruzzi Chapel next door which tell the story of St. John the Baptist and St. John the Evangelist, but these were badly damaged during a horrible restoration in 1841.

The next chapel was owned by the Bonapartes in 1839, and it holds Julie and Charlotte Bonaparte. The sacristy is the large room where the priests prepared for mass and stored vestments.

The frescos in here depict the Life of Christ. These were painted by artists from the Giotto school.

The Rinuccini Chapel frescos were painted by artist and architect Taddio Gaddi who also designed the famous Ponte Vecchio bridge. A hallway leads you to the Medici Chapel, also called the Novitiate Chapel, and to the Dormitory of the Novices built in 1455. To go back into the main church, walk down the corridor.

After coming back into the main church, turn left and follow the outer wall. You will come to Donatello's work, the Annunciation, in the Cavalcanti Chapel. This sculpture is life sized and has a high-relief design which was not commonly used during that time.

This is all that is left of this chapel after Vasari's destructive remodeling project in the year 1560 which was done for the Medici's family wedding to show off Florence to major powers in Europe. All the side chapel walls were removed, frescos whitewashed and replaced with Vassari's large paneled paintings showing the Passion of Christ.

Next is the monument to Niccolo Machiavelli from 1469 to 1527 and author of the book, **The Prince**. He is sometimes referred to as the father of political science. Machiavelli was exiled from Florence, died in 1527, and was not honored until 1787. His epitaph reads, "To a name so great, no praise is equal." His name is often used in reference with the term "Machiavellian" which implies political deceit.

Now we will move on to one of the most famous Florentines! Dante Alighieri, the author of **The Divine Comedy** and also a great political thinker; he is thought to be the father of modern Italian language.

This is only a memorial to Dante. He was exiled and moved to Ravenna where he lived, died, and is buried. Ravenna will not return Dante's remains to Florence. He is shown here sitting with his book at his side along with the figures of Italy and Poetry.

Michelangelo Buonarroti's tomb is next—designed by Vasari, who was a great admirer.

Michelangelo lived from 1475 to 1564. He is the creator of David and painter of the Sistine Chapel in Rome, along with many other accomplisments. On the tomb is a bust of Michelangelo and his own three-ringed emblem. A figure of Painting is on the left, Sculpture is in the center, and Architecture is on the right.

Michelangelo's body is actually buried inside this sarcophagus.

Turn directly behind you to the column, where you will see a bas-relief. This is a form of sculpture which is raised slightly higher with a flat back. This is the Madonna of the Milk from 1478, and she is decorating the floor tomb of Francisco Nori, Lorenzo di Medici's friend.

Look at the carved, beautiful, brocade fabric; how incredible!

Francisco Nori was killed trying to save Lorenzo from a murder attempt during what is called the Pazzi Conspiracy. Lorenzo's brother Giuliano was killed that day. This plan drawn up by the Pazzis, a family of wealthy bankers, who planned to oust the ruling family of the Medicis and then obtain control. This event took place at Easter Day service at the Duomo on April 26, 1478. After this incident began, it was a terrible time for the Medicis, but even worse for the Pazzi family, who were ruined, murdered, and exiled after their murderous plot.

You are also standing very close to a water marker and an indoor wine box, try to find them.

Notice the tomb similar to the Statue of Liberty in the front. Some think this inspired the statue in New York. It looks to me like it could be possible.

The large tomb on the wall directly opposite Michelangelo is the tomb of Galileo Galilei, the famous astronomer who lived from 1564 to 1642. Galileo invented the modern telescope and made many important discoveries which changed the way we looked at the universe. The Medici family appointed him their philosopher and mathematician.

He was originally buried in the Noviate Chapel, because he was not allowed a Christian burial inside the church. In 1633, the Pope did not agree with his theories that the "Earth revolves around the Sun," called heliocentrism.

A Roman Inquisition, or trial, was held, and Galileo was found guilty of heresy, which means his beliefs were against the church. He was then excommunicated from the church and put under house arrest for the last nine years of his life. Ninety-five years later he was finally moved and buried in the main church.

Unbelievably, it was not until 1992 that his excommunication from 1616 was cancelled. This tomb was made in 1737 using a bust of him holding his telescope from 1677. On either side are sculptures representing the figures of Astronomy and Geometry. Galileo's whole body is in here except for two fingers and a thumb which are now housed in the Galileo museum in Florence, an educational experience not to be missed. Some people think his dedicated daughter Maria Celeste may also be buried alongside him.

On the wall near Galileo's tomb, to the right, is a round plaque decorated with circling oak leaves; this is a memorial to Leonardo di Vinci who was born in the town of Vinci and lived and worked in Florence. He is not buried here.

To the left is another memorial to the artist Raphael.

Near the fifth column from the door is the floor tomb of Lorenzo Ghiberti, the creator of the beautiful Baptistery doors. He is buried aside his adopted son Vittorio. Near him, also in the floor, is the tomb of Giorgio Vasari.

Now if you are ready to leave this incredible location containing so many famous people of the Renaissance, please exit through the wooden doors opposite to where you entered and then walk down the stairs into the first cloister. This cloister was used as a graveyard, and during the 19th century the graves where moved into the sidewalls along the colonnade to the left of the stairs. Under the stairway is a door that you can enter to view more graves if you like. Many different water markers are located on the wall along the stairs as this was the main area affected by the many floods.

Follow the beautiful terra cotta, glazed ceiling in the cloister to the Pazzi Chapel. This chapel was built for the Pazzi family and designed by Filippo Brunelleschi. His design is considered to be one of the finest works of Renaissance architecture. The chapel is a work of geometric art using light and dark, and gray and white in a simple elegant design. The chapel was built in 1443 and not was completed until 1478 when the Pazzi family plotted against the Medici's.

Here you will see a series of terra cotta roundels, or round images. The smaller roundels depict the 12 apostles and were created by Luca della Robbia. The larger roundels show the four evangelists. These are attributed to Brunelleschi.

Luca della Robbia and Brunelleschi worked together very often on many different city projects. The Pazzi family emblem of two dolphins is in the corners of the dome. You won't see many of those emblems around town as most were removed after the Pazzis were exiled from Florence.

The second cloister was also designed in Brunelleschi's style but not thought to be designed by him.

Walking further down the colonnade is the Santa Croce Church (OPA) museum where many restored works that were damaged in the 1966 flood are housed. The museum itself was damaged in 1966 and did not reopen until 1975. Many of the frescos that had been detached during Vasari's remodeling project are housed here. There is also a great bookstore.

You can exit though the grassy courtyard directly out into the piazza.

Route One

We are finished with this part of our adventure. I really hope you have greatly enjoyed our day!

The information I have given to you is very brief, but hopefully you have found it interesting and discovered exciting information you wouldn't have otherwise.

Out and About in Florence

Out in the piazza there are many delicious gelato shops and pizzerias where you can take a break. Gelato was invented in Florence in 1565.

And oh, so many shops full of gold. Grab a bench to do some great people watching. Relax now, you've done a lot of scavenging for the day! Enjoy your journey.

Thank you!
Your guide,
Ellen

*Open my heart and you will see,
Engraved inside of it, Italy.*

Robert Browning

Route Two

*A*re you ready to begin a new adventure? We will be experiencing some of the most famous and curious sites of the Renaissance while learning even more about this wondrous time period. The beginning of the Renaissance took place in this very city, which is comparable to none other in the world. We will be traveling to destinations that remain almost exactly as they were hundreds of years ago.

Imagine yourself standing in the very spots where miracles, murder, and treachery took place. Miracles, again? Yes. I will tell you a story of one of the greatest miracles to ever happen; this occurrence changed the entire city!

Remember, you can always break up the journey into different days, or only visit the places that suit your schedule. Let's get started and have some fun taking a journey back though history.

Piazza del Mercato Nuovo and Loggia del Porcellino

Start at the market located on Via S. S. Maria and Piazza Nuovo. Then search for the fountain called Fontana del Porcellino, which means baby piglet,

not what I would have named a large wild boar. It is a bit outside of the Mercato and not directly under the roof. When you find him, there is a ritual to perform to become a true visitor of Florence. First rub his snout, think hard, and make a really good wish. Place a coin into his mouth, and let it drop. If it hits the grate, try again. The coin has to fall though for your wish to come true. It's also a legend that if you rub his nose, you will someday return! I hope this is true! The money collected here goes to local charities.

This open market was built in 1547 for the silk merchants and is called the New Market. In the 13th century, one third of Florence's population were involved in the silk or wool trades. The lamb, holding a crescent-shaped flag in front of the fountain, appears to be a religious symbol but it is not. This is the emblem of the wool guild, Arte de Lana.

Each guild of workers had their own emblem. The Arte de Lana was an extremely powerful guild that contributed to many civic projects. You will notice the lamb everywhere throughout the city.

The Mercato now sells leather goods, scarves, and souvenirs with fairly good prices. Make sure you take the time to find some of your own treasures to take home.

Once inside the market, look at the supporting columns of the roof; one has a very small wooden door. This door opens into a small stairway leading to a large room located under the roof. This room is still used for special events. Wouldn't you love to get up there to see it?!

Now there is something to look for that is very hard to find. Sometimes, actually most times, it is covered by merchandise. It is very easy to locate in the evening when the market is closed, and everyone has cleared out their shops.

This treasure has many names, The Wheel of Carroccio, The Wheel of Shame, and also The Stone of Scandal.

Directly in the center of the market is a marble inlay placed in the floor depicting a Roman chariot wheel. Debtors, people who owed Florence money or taxes, were punished on this wheel. They had to publicly bare their bottoms and were thrown onto this circle.

Ouch! Shame and scandal! This was so horrifying and embarrassing for the person that they would often move from the city. Florence, a city of bankers and international merchants, felt money was a very important matter and no forgiveness was given for unpaid debt.

When you leave, exit onto the Via Porta Rossa at the far end of the market. This is directly opposite the fountain. With the fountain behind you, turn right onto Via Porta Rossa and walk a short block to the street Via del Arte della Lana. Turn left and walk to the church of Orsanmichele. This is the large square building directly ahead. There is a bridge over the road connecting the two buildings.

Orsanmichele

Orsanmichele means the kitchen garden of Saint Michael. It's named after the first church that was built here upon the Garden of St. Michael's Monastery. The church located here now has experienced many curious and unusual circumstances. This is a place where many famous miracles have happened!

The building originally was used for buying

and selling grain. Later it became the church of the guilds. The guilds, or arti, were extremely powerful and eventually became the ruling class of the city. Orsanmichele is an important part of Florence's history. Before we enter the church, let's take a walk around the outside of the building and look at some of its treasures.

The tabernacles, or niches, are holding statues representing the guilds. The carvings, or predellas, are located under the niches, and they can tell us stories. In 1404, the 12 major guilds of Florence were each assigned a niche so they could place a statue of their patron saint in it. Two niches were left open for the Guelph Party, who ran the city during that time. Later these two niches were assigned to the Merchants' Tribunal.

Statues were created by many famous artists including: Donatello, Brunelleschi, Ghiberti, and di Banco. Donatello's famed statue of Saint George, sculpted for the armor and sword makers guild, is now located in the Bargello Museum.

Look for the predella that displays the inside of a horse stable. It was commissioned by the blacksmith and farrier guild.

This carving tells us the story of a miracle; many have taken place here. It is said there was a lame horse that needed to be reshoed. Things were not going well for the horse or the farrier.

The upset horse kicked the barn and knocked off his entire hoof. I don't know if this was the farrier's fault or the horse's. The angry horse then stomped his leg down onto the hoof, and it magically reattached, leaving the horse perfectly happy.

Many different stories are told about this strange incident. One says that horse was the property of the man who owned the granary, and after this miracle, he decided to convert the granary building into a church.

When you walk around the building, hunt for the predella with the image of St. George and the Dragon.

This predella, worked by Donatello, is one of the first carvings done in the bas-relief style, using the art of perspective. The style of perspective gives an illusion of depth within the image. This carving has a foreground, midground, and a background allowing it to appear three dimensional. The art of using perspective was taught to Donatello by Brunelleschi.

Donatello and Brunelleschi were great friends, and they would often travel to Rome searching for ruins to study. Brunelleschi was the famous architect of the dome on the Duomo Cathedral.

One niche displays bronze statues of The Four Crowned Martyrs, done by Nanni di Banco in 1413. These four tell us the story of Christian sculptors who were executed, because they refused to create a statue of a Roman god. Notice how this sculpture is protruding from the niche—also an old classical style.

The entrance to the church is through the doors on the side of the building.

This church holds stories of some of the most spectacular miracles ever to have taken place in Florence!

The original building dated back to 895 and was built on the site of San Michele in Orto; this was demolished in 1239. In 1284, a brick and wood loggia was erected here. A loggia is a walled building with open arches on the sides and has a roof. This building's only purpose was for selling grain. The story of miracles begins in the old loggia. Painted on one of the loggia's pillars was an image of the Madonna of the

Graces. The people of the city thought that miracles would happen at this pillar, and they came to pray to her image, leaving gifts, and lighting candles. The worshippers would arrive in the evening, because the grain market was active during the day. In 1304, due to fighting, there was a large fire in the city, and the loggia was burned. Everything was destroyed except for the pillar that held the Madonna. In 1337, a fireproof, brick granary was started, and completed in 1349. This new building also had an open loggia on the first floor.

The painting of the Madonna was beginning to show her age after time and the fire damage. A new Madonna was commissioned to be painted by Bernardo Daddi in 1337.

The Madonna

The people of Florence came to pray to this painting of the Madonna, to ask her to stop a terrible plague. In 1337, the city's population was around 120,000 people, but a plague in 1340 killed almost 15,000 people—and a famine killed another 4,000. Then, the horrible Black Death arrived in 1348, taking half of the remaining people and leaving the city with only 42,000.

Worshippers thought their prayers to the Madonna cured victims and stopped the plague.

Route Two

A year after the plague ended, a beautiful marble tabernacle was commissioned to hold the image of the Madonna, now known as Madonna delle Grazie, inside the building.

Even though they had to pay money to view the Madonna, they continued to come to pray day and night.

This amazing tabernacle, constructed of swirling marble, lapis, stained glass, and gold, was completed in 1359. It was created by the artist Orcagna, whose name is slang for "archangel." Survivors of the plague paid for the tabernacle, which is one of the most famous artifacts in Florence.

Orcagna's signature and the date are written on its back. Notice how it is located to the side of the building and not in the center aisle as it would be in most churches.

In 1357, the people decided that this building was too important to stay a granary and should be changed into a place of worship. The loggia's arches were filled in 1380, and stained-glass windows were added. You are able to see this from the interior and exterior. In 1404, the brick upper stories were added for storage and the sale of grain. Grain was stored and delivered by a complex method of pulleys and shoots with the rings that are still located on the ceiling.

Sold grain was sent down shoots inside the columns and would travel out to the bases. The church was completed in 1404. To the left of the tabernacle is the altar of St. Anne, who was the mother of the Virgin Mary. St. Anne and St. John the Baptist are both the patron saints of Florence, although St. Anne is an often-forgotten patroness. Above her altar is a very ancient painting with Anne holding the entire city in her arms, still within the city walls.

This church is very special to me because of the amazing miracles said to have happened here. So many people believed in these miracles that they turned a granary into a church!

Upstairs is a wonderful, free museum with incredible views of the city and a spectacular, vaulted, brick ceiling. Most of the original statues, from the outer niches, are now in this museum. There is no fee to enter, but it is only open on Mondays. Sometimes wonderful concerts are held up here in the evening. The ticket office is located outside the main entrance.

When you exit the church, walk ahead on Via Orsanmichele to Via dei Calzaiuoli, make a right turn, and walk straight into the Piazza della Signoria.

Route Two

Piazza della Signoria

The Piazza della Signoria is the heart of Florence, with its civic center and main meeting area. "Signoria" means lordship. This was, and still is, where the Florentine government has its town hall, which is located in the Palazzo Vecchio building, the Salon of 500.

The land here was originally occupied by the Romans; ruins under the Palazzo Vecchio have been found.

In the year 1000, this entire area you are in was filled with fortified tower houses, which were mostly owned by one family, the Ubertis. They were supporters of the Ghibelline political party who were at war with the Guelphs. The Ghibellines supported the Holy Roman Emperor and the

Guelphs supported the Pope. Among other conflicts, this caused many disagreements including the Black and White War. This war lasted for almost 200 years.

They lived in and fought from these 200-foot-tall, square, brick towers. Can you imagine towers of that height? Wooden bridges connected neighboring towers and were pulled up during fighting. Wooden balconies hung on the outside walls of the towers, which were built closely together for more protection, and they were gathered into neighborhoods.

The tower height was very beneficial for dropping rocks and boiling liquids below; even people not involved with these arguments were in great danger when leaving home. In 1256, the fighting was still going on. A law was enforced stating a tower could not be over 90-feet tall. So, the towers were cut down to that height. I've read there were enough bricks left to build the city wall.

At the end of the 1200s, the Guelphs finally won the war during a huge battle and the owners of the Ghibelline towers were exiled from Florence forever. The towers they owned were torn down, and the land they had stood on was cursed!

This land was never to be lived on again. All this drama occurred in this Piazza.

The tower on the Palazzo Vecchio, the large brick building, is named Della Vacca, or the Cow's Tower. It received its name, because the bells sound like a cow mooing. The Foraboschi family's existing tower was reused

on the Palazzo Vecchio. The Della Vacca tower was eventually raised to its current height of 328 feet. The bell was used to call citizens to meetings and alert people of impending floods and wars. The Bargello's Volognana tower is another saved building which was incorporated into the old city prison. If you climb up the Palazzo Vecchio tower, you will be able to walk around the protruding crenelated ramparts 131 feet above the piazza. You can view the height from the cutouts in the floor. These were used for the pouring of hot liquids onto adversaries. During your climb up the tower, visit the Alberghetto, or little hotel, that was a prison for many years. The visit to the tower requires a separate ticket. When you are at any high point looking down upon the city, you will be able to see many towers standing alone and others that have been built into their current structures. After noticing a few, you will start seeing them everywhere. Some have brown signs marking them at street level.

In 1298, the Priori, or Signoria, who were then the rulers of the city and bearers of justice planned to enlarge the meeting area inside the Palazzo Vecchio. At this time the building was called Palazzo Popolo—the palace of the people. The enlargement was completed in 1302. The oldest portion of the building has the crenellated top. The government and city grew larger, and the building again became too small. The piazza was also shrinking, and everything needed to be expanded. It took almost 100 years for the city to purchase

enough property surrounding the piazza so the enlargement could be completed. This is why the piazza has such an odd shape; it is a trapezoid instead of a square. At the end of the 14th century, the piazza was paved and all heavy traffic was banned.

    A large church was located between the Palazzo Vecchio and where the Uffizi museum is now. This church took up too much space in the corner of the piazza and stood in the way of progress. The church was on the Via della Ninna. "Ninna" is the Italian word for lullaby. This is the very narrow street with a walkway above connecting the two buildings. If you are facing the Palazzo Vecchio, the Via della Ninna will be to your right. The church was San Pier Scheraggio and built around 1068 over an older church from the 9th century. At the time it was one of the largest in the city, but all of it was entirely demolished, except for one outer wall and two naves which are now part of the Uffizi building. Services were held in the two naves until the 1700s. Look for its old arches and pillars built into the Uffizi's outer wall. If you go into neighboring shops, you will see some of its remains inside.

   A plaque placed high on the Uffizi's or San Pier Scheraggio's wall reads, "Within these walls, Dante's voice rang out in the people's councils." Long ago, Dante and the author Boccaccio would often speak in the old church.

   From the church's wall, walk ahead to the front corner of Palazzo Vecchio. Look behind the large statue of Hercules clubbing Cacus. There is an image and profile of a head carved directly into the wall of the building by the artist Michelangelo. I've heard three different stories about this carving. One story explains there was a bet to see if Michelangelo was able to carve with one arm behind his back. A second story indicates that he saw a prisoner on his way to the gallows, and he wanted to quickly capture his expression.

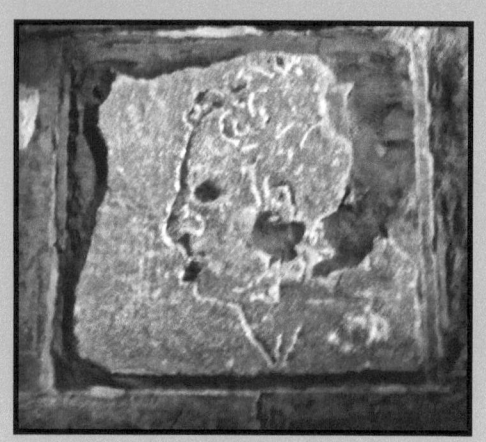

   A third offers the explanation that he was bored

listening to someone who was talking to him and just started carving away on the building wall.

As you look behind you, notice the stunning arched open building containing all the beautiful sculptures.

This is the Loggia dei Lanzi, originally called Loggia della Signoria.

Be sure to walk over there. This elegant building with its three graceful arches is an open-air sculpture museum. Lanzi, or Lanzichenecchi, were the German mercenary guards who the Medici family had hired for protection. Built between 1376

and 1382, it was used for ceremonies held by the government.

When the guards were no longer needed for protection the Loggia was turned into an open sculpture area—a very nice idea on the Medici's part. Along the upper portion are trefoil-shaped paintings with images of the four virtues, Fortitude, Temperance, Justice, and Prudence.

A rooftop area was added later for the Medici's personal use, and it is now the café for the Uffizi Gallery museum. It provides yet another spectacular view of the city.

Take a good look at the statues in the Loggia and the Piazza; can you see the artwork's theme?

It's a pretty tough place! It seems as if everyone is fighting, getting ready to fight, or has just finished. It's all very brutal—heads chopped off, clubs taken out, and women being carried away. This is a very masculine place— not fancy or frilly like Venice.

Lions, which are another symbol

of Florence, are seen everywhere. In the Loggia, hundreds line the back wall. Do you think these were hooks for the Lanzi to hang their weapons on? Florence kept live lions on the spot where the Loggia de Lanzi stands until 1300. They were well taken care of and were always watched. They quickly reproduced and grew in number from two to 24. In 1350, the lions were moved to the Via de Lioni and kept there for 200 years. Via de Lioni is  located on the left side of Palazzo Vecchio. Kept in cages, they were observed during times of crisis to see how they would react. It was felt they could see into the future. They were moved again during Duke Cosimo's remodeling of the area.

The art in the Piazza and Loggia is meant to be a civics lesson for the citizens and a warning for the city's enemies. The sculptures in the Loggia are originals; some are very old Greek and Roman works.

Inside the Loggia is a plaque stating the name of the artist and year of each piece. Also displayed are descriptions containing the meanings of each work. This is a spectacular place to come in the evening, the statues and buildings are all lit against the dark night sky.

The Statue of Perseus

This bronze statue created by Benvenuto Cellini, the famous goldsmith, was started in 1549 and completed in 1554. This is probably the most famous in the Loggia. Created in the Italian Mannerist style, this was a very difficult piece to cast. Perseus is holding up the cut off head of Medusa, an evil monster with dangerous live snakes instead of hair. The myth states that Danae, a mortal, was showered in a spray of gold by the god Zeus, and she then gave birth to Perseus. The two were sent away. When Perseus was grown, the local king ordered him to kill the Gorgon Medusa. Medusa was not born a monster; she was once a beautiful, young maiden with long, flowing hair. A very jealous goddess cursed Medusa, and she

Route Two

became a Gorgon; she was so terrifying that if anyone looked at her, they turned into stone. Perseus wore the helmet of Hades, which offered him the protection of invisibility, and he had a

sword from the god Mercury. He snuck up behind Medusa and killed her while she was alone praying to the gods to end her misery.

This statue is the original, commissioned by Duke Cosimo I in 1554. Cosimo wanted this statue to be a strong political warning to his enemies, showing them the strength of Florence. The marble base of Perseus is also very beautiful and tells the story of his life. It exhibits his father Zeus, mother Danae, along with Perseus, and his siblings, Minerva and Mercury.

There is a very strange, secret surprise on Perseus! Look at the back of the statue. Cast into the back of the helmet is a self-portrait of the artist Cellini. Interestingly enough, he did not include this image on his smaller model which was submitted for approval to the Medici's. That smaller statue is now in the Bargello Museum without an image on the back of the helmet.

Now turn toward the Piazza, and walk to the statue of Duke Cosimo seated on a horse. He is shown as a Roman emperor going into battle, and it was done by Giambologna in 1595 on a commission by Cosimo's son.

The very large fountain is called Fontana di Neptuno, Il Biancone, or the Great White Man. Unveiled on December 10, 1574, it was the first public fountain in the city. A competition was held for the design of a fountain showing Florence's maritime power.

The artist Bartolomeo Ammannati won the design competition.

Neptune is shown frolicking with his sea creatures surrounded by horses, shells, and Zodiac symbols. When Il Biancone was presented to the citizens of Florence, they had a horrible opinion of him and said, "Oh, what a great waste of marble."

Now, again, I have another amazing story of myths and miracles. This story is about the fountain Il Biancone. Legend says he was originally a man but was turned into a stone statue because he did not love women. Supposedly, when a full moon shines upon him at midnight, but only at midnight, he will come to life and walk the Piazza speaking to all the other statues. He must have known I was watching him at midnight, during a full moon, because I definitely did not see him move.

Look for a circular, metal plaque laid flat into the pavement; this plaque marks where the Bonfire of the Vanities took place. Later, on this very same spot Friar Girolamo Savonarola, who held the bonfire, was hung and burned to death. Savonarola was a Dominican monk who told the citizens that he received visions from God in which he could foresee the future and warn of such things as plague and war. He was lucky, and a few times he guessed fairly close, so people believed him.

Savonarola became extremely popular with many followers. In 1497, when he wanted people to repent for their sins and vanities, he ordered all Florentines to pile up their jewels, art, fine clothing, and luxury items on this very spot. The heap reached an enormous height, and then it was all set on fire.

How many precious pieces of artwork, do you think, were consumed by the flames? The artist Botticelli was a follower of Savonarola's; what masterpieces might he have thrown in?

In 1497, the Pope excommunicated Savonarola because of his wild preaching, but he still did not stop. He was finally arrested and had a trial by ordeal, which involved walking on fire, the rack, and other horrifying means of torture. Savonarola then was accused of heresy and condemned to death along with two of his disciples, who were called Piagnoni or "The Weepers." After being tortured in the Bargello prison for many days, on May 23, 1498, he was put to death. It was ordered he be hung very, very slowly and then burned on the same spot where his fire was held. After his burning, which was done twice, his ashes were thrown into the Arno River so he would not be able to have a Christian burial and be thought a martyr.

In the front of the Palazzo Vecchio on the ledge is Donatello's Marzocco Heraldic Lion. The Marzocco Lion is Florence's protector and the symbol of justice. "Marzocco" comes from the Latin word Martius or Mars, the god of war. Holding a shield with the lily emblem of Florence on it, the lion is life-size and meant to be terrifying or "Terribilitia." The original sculpture is now located in the Bargello museum. Some shields on other Marzoccos in the city carry the quote, "I wear the crown for our deserving land, that freedom is maintained in every hand." Next to the lion is another copy of a work by Donatello that features Judith slaying Holofernes. The original is now inside the Palazzo Vecchio. The statue was part of a large fountain at the Medici family home—Palazzo Medici. The people removed it from Palazzo Medici during a short time while the family was in exile. Look to see if you can spot the water spigots!

David

Michelangelo was commissioned by the wool guild in 1501 to create a statue of David for the façade of the Duomo. The statue of David is based on the biblical story of a shepherd, David, who slays the giant Goliath with only a slingshot. David is the Florentine civic symbol of Republican Freedom.

There certainly are many symbols throughout this city. David is shown standing strong preparing for his battle. This statue was carved from a single piece of imperfect marble that had been worked on and abandoned by another artist.

Michelangelo was only 29 years old when he started his David.

It's amazing how someone so young was so gifted in creating such an incredible masterpiece. Michelangelo worked on the statue of David in his workshop, which was located where the Museo dell Opera is now. For three years he would not let anyone view his work. David was completed on September 8,

Out and About in Florence

1504, and stands 16 feet tall. When finished, there was a great debate about where to place him. It was decided that the statue would not be placed on the Duomo façade as originally planned, but instead would be placed on this very spot in the Piazza. With the work of 40 men, it took four days to move the statue from Michelangelo's studio as it was transported upright and did not touch the ground. The David standing guard here today is a copy of the original, which is now located in the Galleria dell' Accademia along with other great works by Michelangelo, such as The Slaves. The original statue stood in this piazza until 1873. It was then decided that he needed to be moved indoors for protection from the environment.

Poor David has had a few accidents in his life. In 1512, the base of the David statue was hit by lightning. In 1521, his left arm was broken off during a political revolt. This revolt took place inside the Palazzo Vecchio. A bench was thrown out of the window, and it fell onto David, breaking his arm. If you visit the Galleria dell' Accademia and look carefully, you really can see where his arm was broken and then repaired. In 1813, one finger was broken, and in 1843 one toe was broken. In 1991, while he was located in the Accademia, his foot was smashed with a hammer by a museum worker.

If you have time, please visit the Galleria dell' Accademia to view the original David. This work is one of absolute amazement and is placed in a specially designed dome displaying his beauty. It is worth the effort and time waiting in line to view one of the greatest works in the history of art.

Next to David, to the right of the entrance, is the statue of Hercules and Cacus by Bandinelli from 1534.

Hercules is brutally punishing Cacus, Vulcan's son, with a club for stealing four cows and four bulls from him.

Statues of Adam and Eve flank the doorway.

You can enter the building's beautiful, elaborate courtyard though the doorway next to David. You will also see, on the blue portal above the entrance, two lions guarding Christ's monogram. The ornate central courtyard was redone in 1560 and is adorned with frescoed walls, carved pillars, and a very cute putto fountain. A puttos is an image of a young, nude male with wings, and are usually associated with Eros or Cupid. The plural of putto is putti, and there are many of them all over the Palazzo. This little putto is a copy. The original, by Andrea del Verrocchio, is an important piece of renaissance sculpture because it can be viewed from all angles; it is now located in an apartment on the second floor.

To view the rest of the Palazzo Vecchio, you will need to purchase a ticket from the office on the first floor. Many different tours are available throughout the building.

Let me give you some information on the building, which you can use whether you go inside or not. If you do go in, you will not be disappointed. You will be given a brochure with your ticket that includes important information, so I won't repeat it all to you here. Start at the Palazzo's main room, called the Hall of the 500 or Salone dei Cinquecento. Girolamo Savonarola, the friar who was burned, wanted a large space where 500 wise men could meet to rule alongside the government during the Medici's exile. The building was enlarged in 1494 to create this room. Florence's ruling party was a council of nine men, called the Priori Signoria. Six represented the major guilds, and two represented the minor guilds. A ninth man, the Gonfaloniere, was the temporary bearer of the city's banner, and he held the most important position.

    These men were selected by a drawing. To qualify, the man must be a guild member, at least 30 years old, and without any debt. Remember, debt was a very bad thing to have in Florence. Candidate's names were put into eight leather bags called "borse," then randomly selected. Those who had recently served were disqualified. The nine men served for two months in the Palazzo Vecchio without their families and were isolated so they would not be influenced by current events. They lived in the apartments along with male attendants. Prioris wore red cloaks and caps which you can see in many Florentine paintings. The Gonfaloniere had golden stars embroidered onto his robe. The Medici's returned in 1512 from their 1494 exile after Savonarola's execution. Duke Cosimo I de Medici lived for a short time in the Medici palace near San Lorenzo. The family later decided to move into the Palazzo della Signoria, now the Palazzo Vecchio. The Duke and his wealthy young wife, Eleonora di Toledo, took over the Priori's apartments in 1540. Giorgio Vasari was commissioned at this time to remodel the entire Palazzo.

The Grand Duke was a great man who was interested in architecture, science, music, and agriculture. He also was a patron supporting local artists, writers, and scholars, and he recruited them to work in his magnificent city. The entire city of Florence is a World UNESCO heritage site and contains almost 60 percent of the world's greatest treasures of art. The Galleria degli Uffizi is most assuredly worth a visit; there is nowhere in the world comparable to its holdings. It is best to purchase your ticket in advance of your visit and avoid the line. Arrive early, as you may want to spend many hours admiring its treasures. The gallery is closed on Mondays and open later some evenings. The Medicis commissioned Vasari to design the building as their Palace of Offices in the 16th century. In 1765, it was opened as an art museum to showcase the family's collections.

When leaving the courtyard of Palazzo Vecchio, return to the small street Via del Ninna. As you look up, you will see a small bridge spanning the street. This is the starting point of the Vasari Corridor, or the Prince's Passage.

The corridor, in case you haven't guessed, was designed and built by Vasari in 1564 for the wedding of Cosimo and Eleonora's son. Vasari was working everywhere during this time. The corridor starts at Palazzo Vecchio and ends at what was then the Medici's new residence: the Pitti Palace. Eleonora purchased the unfinished Palace, from the bankrupt Pitti family, and it would need a few years to be completed.

But Eleonora died young, in 1562, from malaria and never was able to take residence at their new home. The elevated passageway, which is one kilometer in length, was built for the family. It was used to safely travel back and forth so as not to be seen amongst the people—especially for fear of assassination. Vasari called it, "The run through," or "Just a way out." It was also a wonderful way to spy on the public.

Tickets are available for small group tours.

After crossing over Via de Ninni, the corridor follows an upper gallery hallway in the Uffizi which leads to a pair of doors that open and lead down a stairway, becoming very private. It is all gray and white with high ceilings and small, round, grated windows. The corridor holds an impressive collection of almost 1,000 paintings— all self-portraits by famous artists throughout history, including many modern artists. Walk along the Uffizi toward the river, and follow the route of the Vasari Corridor. Many statues of famous Florentines are along the sides; this walkway, between buildings, is the Uffizi Corridor. Stop at the railing along the river at the end.

The Corridor then goes over the Lungarno, which means along the Arno River. The Vasari Corridor is hiding above the walkway with the large arches.

Standing at the railing next to the river and looking toward the Ponte Vecchio bridge, you can see two grated windows as the corridor exits the Uffizi and enters under the tiled roof of the walkway.

Turn right and follow under the walkway towards

the bridge. This is the Lungarno. The Lungarno becomes the Via Anna Maria Luisa de Medici.

Anna Maria was the last surviving Medici. She donated all of the Medici's property to the city of Florence in 1737. A huge gift to the city as well as to all people of the world! What would Florence be without this gift?

On the Via Anna Maria, at the Ponte Vecchio bridge, the Vasari Corridor turns and crosses the river above the bridge.

When you are walking, turn left onto this historic bridge and stop in the center for

a minute so I can show you the rest of the corridor and tell you some details about the bridge. Butchers and tanneries were  the businesses in the shops along the bridge at the time the corridor was built. The prince felt these merchants created very nasty odors, and he forced

 them to move out. Then, he invited goldsmiths to replace their shops. The center windows in the corridor above the bridge were replaced with the larger ones in 1939 by Mussolini.

This was done to show off the view of the Arno to Adolf Hitler during World War II.

The corridor protrudes and wraps around the Mannelli Tower at the end of the bridge on the opposite side of the river. Vasari had purchased all the property along the walkway except for this one tower. The Mannelli family refused to sell and move. The tower was the last remaining of the four originally built to guard the bridge, and they stood firm that it should be left. The Florentines and Cosimo di Medici agreed with the family and the Mannelli's tower was kept.

A design was made for the corridor to run along the outside of the tower on side supports. As you look up, you will be able to notice this. Leaving the tower, the corridor continues to run along Via de Bardi, where it goes through the church, Santa Felicita, and blocks some of the church's façade.  Inside the church, there is an opening onto an upper balcony which let the Medici's attend their religious services privately. The corridor then makes another turn and ends at the Pitti Palace—the Medici's new home. There is a hidden exit door in a grotto of the Pitti Gardens; a grotto is a small, artificial, decorative cave. The corridor fully ends at the palace, and its total length is about half a mile.

Ponte Vecchio in Italian means the "Old Bridge." It crosses the Arno River at its lowest point. A Roman encampment called Florentia, meaning the flourishing town, was established in 59 B.C. as a retirement camp for war veterans. The Romans built a wooden bridge here, and on its northern corner they placed a statue of their patron, Mars the god of war. A flood destroyed the bridge, and it was rebuilt.

The rebuilt bridge was destroyed in the flood of 1333; during that flood the statue of Mars was swept away and never found.

The bridge was rebuilt in 1345, and it is the very one you are standing on right now—a very old bridge that has been through much. Taddeo Gaddi designed this bridge with its three stone arches sitting on heavy piers allowing it to cut the water and ease the flow of the river. Large openings allow rushing water and debris to flow though during a flood.

Shops line both sides with a throughway in the center. Since the goldsmiths arrived, the bridge feels like a giant sparkling jewelry box. In the center, you will find the bust of Florence's most famous goldsmith, Benvenuto Cellini, the creator of the statue of Perseus. While walking around the bridge, search its stone walls for many rectangular carved images of ancient towers. Do you think they represent the three towers torn down?

Also look at the shop's rooftops, and try to find an ancient sundial sitting upon a white marble pillar. When you find it, the writing underneath states, "In the year of 1333, the bridge collapsed due to floods of water and 12 years later as pleased the Commune it was rebuilt with this ornamentation."

Also at the end of the arched walkway that brought you to the bridge, you will see a Dante

Plaque. There are 34 of these plaques throughout the city, containing quotes from Dante's **La Divina Commedia**—*nine are from the Inferno, five are from Purgatorio, and 20 are from the book Paradiso.*

These plaques are all placed at the spots in which they are mentioned in his books. This plaque is located on a very important site! It is marking the spot where Buondelmonte de' Buondelmonti didn't commit to a planned marriage with a member of the important Amidei family. Riding past this spot on Easter Day in 1215, on his way to marry his real true love, the upset Amidei family had him brutally murdered. This incident started the civil war

between the blacks and whites, or the Guelphs and Ghibellines, which lasted almost 200 years. Written on the plaque is an excerpt from Dante's book,

which speaks of Florence's last day of peace, which happened at the statue of Mars.

The views from the bridge are some of the most beautiful in the entire city. This is also a wonderful place for viewing the sunset.

 We have now arrived at the end of this Treasure Hunt. There are many stunning things out in the open, but there is also much hiding from you.

 Florence holds its hidden treasures and secrets everywhere. This city is comparable to no other in the world; it is the only place you can experience these wonders. You are very fortunate to have come here, and I hope you will always have good memories of our day together.

 But before we part, there is one more Treasure Hunt starting at the Oltrarno point of the bridge. Oltrarno means the other side of the Arno. If you cross the river there are many excellent restaurants, or you can walk up to a food counter and get a panini to take away. Old neighborhoods with craftsmen's shops, stores, and quaint wine patios await you along the way.

Thank you for letting me accompany you on our past adventure. Our next adventure is actually a search for the best view of Florence from above. The views and walking out of the main city are breathtaking. This route is also much shorter.

I'm looking forward to another great adventure in beautiful Florence with you!

          Ellen

Italy is a dream that keeps returning for the rest of your life.

Anna Akhmatova

Route Three

To Piazza Michelangelo and the Church of San Miniato al Monte

Hello everyone,

On our new journey, we will discover the best views in all of Florence. We will spend time exploring many fascinating locations in the Oltrarno area of the city; "Oltrarno" means the other side of the Arno River. Piazza Michelangelo is famously known for its fantastic views, but we will also explore other sites which share equal or even more exceptional vistas. You will view Florence from above as we walk and discover our treasures. You will have two walking options to choose from, both will lead you to our first location—the Piazza Michelangelo. This is the only difference in our journey.

One walk is a bit more challenging and will take you slightly longer. Just a short hike uphill will lead you through an ancient part of the city which holds small houses and tiny, winding, arched streets. This option will also take you through an old city gate. The other walking option, to the Piazza Michelangelo, is also very nice but easier and much shorter. It's the best option if you are limited on time.

If you are up for the second walk and have the time, I suggest this option. Along the way, there is a beautiful rose garden where you can rest on a bench and take in the incredible view of Florence. There are also quite a few nice places to stop for a bite or enjoy a drink, otherwise everything else on this journey is free.

Route Three

The quick route up to the Piazza Michelangelo

If you begin where we left off on our last adventure, stand at the end of the Ponte Vecchio Bridge, and with your back to the bridge, turn left. Walk along the side of the river; this is called the Oltrarno, or other side of the Arno.

Next, turn right into the Piazza Giuseppe Poggi, and you will see the huge tower, Porta San Niccolo. This tower from 1324 was used as a gate and a defense building—part of the old fortress walls. Of the 13 city towers, this was the only one not lowered in 1530 because it was still used for protection of the hill. Opposite, across the river, the Mint Tower stands. In the arch above the gate is a fresco of the Virgin and Child.

Follow up the Poggi's ramp straight up to the piazza. Along the walls there are interesting Grottos with small pools. A grotto is a small, artificial, decorative cave. When we arrive at the Piazza, let's take in the amazing scenery and wait for the other travelers to arrive.

The second route up to the Piazza Michelangelo

We will start this beautiful journey at the end of the Ponte Vecchio Bridge. You will then be in the Oltrarno, which means the other side of the Arno River.

With your back to the bridge, turn to your left. Follow onto the Via de Bardi, and then cross the road at Piazza di Santa Maria Soprarno. Next follow onto the Costa Dei Magnoli, then turn left onto the Via Vicolo del Cantreto. This all sounds somewhat confusing, but it is a very short distance and easy to follow. Walk up the hill under the arch but do not take the stairs to your right. Soon you will enter a charming old part of the city with narrow, stone-paved, turning streets and covered arches as well as very quaint homes. As you wind though these narrow streets, you will feel as if you were lead back in time.

As you walk, you will come to Costa Scarpuccia Street which shortly returns to the Via Bardi at the intersection of Bardi and Piazza Mozzi. Continue walking straight ahead.

DON'T worry, there will be large brown street signs that will direct you straight into the Piazza.

Here there are many places to grab a bite to eat or enjoy a glass of wine. You could also get carryout and eat it at our next stop, which contains a beautiful view, the rose garden park.

Next, walk through the old city gate, or Port San Miniato, which is still connected to its historical city walls. Walking ahead, go to the wide stairway which displays the Stations of the Cross along the side wall.

Before you ascend the stairs, look around before you ascend the stairs for another Dante plaque. It sometimes hides under the ivy.

At the base of the stairs, you will most likely find merchants selling reasonably priced souvenirs.

Halfway up the stairs, you will come to a wide landing, turn left, and enter the public rose garden, the Giardino della Rose. This garden is a special secret. It's a quiet, peaceful park and home to over 350 different varieties of roses. There are benches, walkways, and fantastic views of Florence. This is a wonderful spot to relax and have a picnic, away from the bustle of the city.

After you have taken in the views and rested, then return to the stairs, which will lead you directly up to Piazza Michelangelo.

Now we have all arrived in the Piazza Michelangelo, which is said to have the most

spectacular views in all of Florence—showcasing panoramic scenes of the city and countryside from its point on the hill. Standing proudly in the center of the Piazza is a 16-foot-tall replica of Michelangelo's David, surrounded by copies of the statues he designed for the Medici Chapel in San Lorenzo Church. These four statues depict: Night, Day, Dusk, and Dawn.

What an incredible view!

Route Three

A loggia, located to the side of the piazza, was originally intended to become a museum but never transpired. It is now a very nice restaurant to visit.

Enjoy walking around the entire edge and taking in the gorgeous scenery of the city, the river, and country hills. To the left are remnants of the old city wall snaking up the hill. Usually there are some vendors here selling souvenirs; many are copies of the David statue. See if you can find a good likeness, as some are not done in the best taste.

Out and About in Florence

San Miniato al Monte

When you have finished here, walk across the piazza and go to the main road.

Please be very careful here when you cross this street! After carefully crossing, walk to the right and follow the brown signs leading you up the hill named Monte alle Croci. This will bring us to the church, San Miniato del Monte, which is located on the highest point in the city. This church is said  to be one of the most scenic in the world, and one of Florence's most important pieces of architecture.

Climb the impressive wide stairway to reach this ancient masterpiece. At the top, you will be able to look down you and see far and wide. This, I feel, is the most beautiful view of the entirety of Florence!

Don't you think this was well worth the climb?

The land surrounding the church contains a large cemetery named the Cimitero Monumental delle Porte. Here, there are very unique grave

markers, statues, and individual ornate mausoleums at the rear. Many famous Florentines are here. It's worth a look around.

This area is surrounded by walls that Michelangelo built to protect his properties during a siege. The Campanile Tower collapsed in 1499 and was rebuilt in 1523. During this siege, the fortified tower was wrapped with mattresses to protect it. You can see the cannon marks that were fired upon it. After viewing the church, please take a walk through the cemetery; it is very interesting! There is also a small store which sells souvenirs and items made by the friars.

The ancient church of San Miniato was built in 1018 over 4th century Roman ruins. Olivetan Friars took over the church from the Benedictines in 1373. The friars still live in the monastery located in the building to the side of the church. In the afternoon, you will hear them singing 1000-year-old Gregorian chants. It is extremely moving and allows you to almost transcend into another time period.

Here is yet another story about a very early and important miracle—the story of San Minias who was Florence's first local martyr. It is said that in the 3rd century, Minias, an Armenian prince who had served in the Roman Army, was denounced as a Christian, which was a crime at the time. This was because he was living his life in a cave as a hermit. He was thrown into the amphitheater, near where Santa Croce is located now, and he was to be killed by beasts. The beasts did not want to kill him, and became peaceful. So, after not having been eaten, it was then ordered that he was to be decapitated in the arena. He was decapitated! It's said that after this happened, he picked up his head and ran across the Arno River back up the mountain to the cave where he had been living.

A shrine was built on this site; then, in the 8th century, a chapel was also constructed.

The church that stands here now was started in 1013 on the same location. San Miniato's Romanesque green and white marble façade was designed to match the Baptistery.

The church's lower portion has five arches and two false doors. The doorway on the left is the Holy Portal, and on its threshold is an inscription stating, "This is the Gate of Heaven" (Genesis, 28:17). Above the entrance, there is a rectangle holding glittering,

golden glass mosaics showing the images of Christ, Mary, and Saint Minias. Look for a small triangle with two doves. Notice the elaborate carvings with lions supporting their sides. The edges along the façade are decorated with small medieval heads. The large bronze eagle on the very top corner is the symbol of the cloth merchants' guild, which was in charge of maintaining the church. During an earthquake in 1895, the eagle fell through the roof.

The Nave

The first thing you will notice when entering though the doors will be the nave, or main aisle. Here is incredible tile work which is also similar to the Baptistery. This part of the church's original decoration is worked in an old style called Intarsia, which was popular during Roman times. Here is one more large round "Zodiac of Life" divided into 12 sections thought to represent the 12 apostles. Above this design are tiled gryphons, dragons, birds, and other imaginary beasts. The remainder of the floor was removed in 1770 during a fundraiser which allowed followers and family to be buried into the floor.

The free-standing tabernacle at the side of the aisle, or nave, also holds an eagle on its top. It is

"The Chapel of the Crucifix" from 1448.

Inside, it held a beautiful crucifix which is now housed in the Church of Santa Trinita. This crucifix was said to hold pieces of the true cross. The upper portion was created by the terra cotta artist della Robbia.

To the left, in the vault, is a tomb which also has more terra cotta decoration by Luca della Robbia. As you look up, notice the painted trussed ceiling from 1322.

Decorations

Upstairs the unusual raised choir platform contains a very amazing pulpit, or ambo from 1207. Look at the serious little medieval monk standing on top of a lion with an eagle on his head. Notice his glass eyes; don't you just love him?! All around the choir screen are interesting little imaginary medieval creatures and humans dancing along the edges.

Route Three

The Apse

In the apse, or area, at the end of the nave, is a large, sparkling, golden Byzantine-style mosaic. This is of Christ, Mary, and Saint Minias. Also represented are the four Evangelists, the Apostles in a ring, and a Phoenix in flames with other birds. The altar from 1394, by Agnolo Gaddi, shows Saint Minias dressed in an oriental robe. The windows in the lower apse are opaque and made of very thin alabaster, representing "The Sun of Christ that rises in the Orient." They look incredible; when the sun hits them, they appear to be on fire. The wall frescos along the stairs were done by many different artists throughout time. There is more information in the church regarding these artists. On the second floor, to the right, is the sacristy, showing large frescos worked in Giotto's style, telling the story of Saint Benedict. Do you see the Devil holding down the stone?

The Crypt

In the lower level, there is a serene area which contains the crypt. This is the oldest area of the church. This vaulted room is where early Christians were buried. The high altar is said to hold the remains of San Minias, but this has been debated for years. Take a seat in this ancient area, and study the 38 slender columns including the smaller ones around the vault.

Most are carved differently as they are reused Roman pieces. The ceiling fresco was painted by Taddio Gaddi who was also the designer of the Ponte Vecchio bridge.

As you walk out of the church and onto the terrace, admire this captivating view of the entire city.

This is my favorite place to gaze upon the city of Florence.

When you leave, hopefully after visiting the unique cemetery, return down the stairs. Then turn *right, and follow the brown signs back to Piazza Michelangelo. At the piazza take a last look at the beautiful city of Florence! As you face the Duomo, walk across the piazza to your right and descend down the Poggi walkway leading to the tower. If you are heading back to the Ponte Vecchio bridge, turn left facing the river and walk along the Lungarno, or cross the nearest bridge and you will be close to Santa Croce church and piazza.*

I have so enjoyed sharing my information of the city of Florence with you. I am wishing you many more journeys to unknown places and new explorations in your future!

*Your happy guide,
Ellen*

Things To Look For During Your Adventure

Here are some very interesting things to search for while you are walking during your adventure. There are many things hiding right before you that you may not notice if you don't realize what they are. Remember you need to search up, down, and all around!

Arno Flood Markers

These are located all over the city, inside churches, on piazza walls and on buildings. These are the high water level markers noting the rising height of the Arno River during floods. Many of the markers are located on corners, so you will need to look up. Try to imagine the height of the water.

Fifty-six floods in the city where recorded since the year 1178. Major floods occurred in 1269; November 4, 1333; 1466; 1557; November 3, 1844; September 8, 1857; and November 4, 1844. Strangely, the two major floods both occurred on November 4. The markers are in done in many different styles due to the year of the flood.

Things To Look For During Your Adventure

Buchette de Vino or Little Wine Hole

Here is something intriguing to find. Wine Holes! In the past when the city's economy was declining families living in the city who also owned vineyards would sell their wine though these small doors. They received extra income without the taxes. Customers would bring their flask to be filled and put it though the door. During times of plague they were also used. During the COVID-19 pandemic, they were put to use again. See how many you can spot!

Things To Look For During Your Adventure

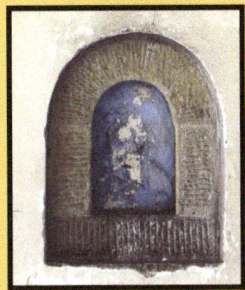   

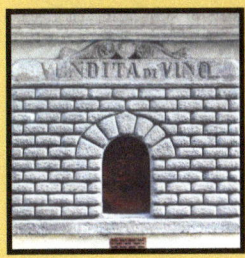   

Dante Plaques

There are 34 carved stone plaques throughout the city. These are placed in locations that correlate with the specific canto, or verse, in Dante's **La Divina Commedia**, his most famous work. Dante scholars took 7 years to place them.

9 are from "The Inferno"
5 are from "Purgatorio"
20 are from "Paradiso"

Dante Alighieri was born in Florence in 1265. At that time, it was more common for authors to write in Latin, even if they spoke a different language. By writing in Italian, Dante helped to established the written Italian language.

Things To Look For During Your Adventure

Prohibit

This word is carved into buildings all through the city. They mark laws prohibiting things such as ball playing, prostitution, or large gatherings. One is near the fountain of Neptune declaring no laundry to be done there.

Tower Houses

While you are walking or viewing from above, you can see many square-shaped brick buildings. These are the Tower homes that had been lopped off when it was ruled that no building could be higher than the Palazzo Vecchio. They are everywhere; many have a brown sign with a tower marking them at street level.

Cross the Ponte Vecchio bridge, and turn right to San Jacopo St., and you can find a whole neighborhood of them.

Things To Look For During Your Adventure

Tabernacles

These are small religious shrines which are mostly located on corners and the sides of buildings. Many represent the Madonna, and have been popula,r since 1200, as a place to walk by and pray, or as a display of a show of wealth.

During times of plague, they were used by nearby residents to pray at so they would not have to attend a crowded church.

Florence had many plagues!
1340: Plague killed one sixth of the population.
1348: Plague took half the population.
There were plagues in 1402, 1430, 1438, 1450, and 1530.
In 1336, it became legal to import foreigners who would be forced to be slaves due to the lack of domestic servants.

Family Emblems- Cartouches

Families designed emblems to mark their homes or businesses and projects they had invested in. Finding and decoding the Medici emblem can be confusing! Its number of balls, or Palle, is not fixed, and family members would often add their wives' family emblem to the side.

Here is a short story about how the Medici emblem came to be...

The Medicis were descended from a brave knight named Averardo, who fought under Charlemagne. While Averardo was riding though the north of Florence he came upon a huge giant. Averardo fought him so the citizens of Florence would be safe. He killed him. During his battle his shield was badly dented from the giant's mace. As a reward Charlemagne allowed him to show his victory over the giant by giving him an emblem representing the dents with palle. These were red with a golden background. In 1378, the Medici family was not very popular, and it was said this story was false. It was then said that the palle represented the pills of a lowly apothecary, or a charcoal burner.

How many can you find?
Make a checkmark when you do.

Glossary

Arti - These were the Guilds of Florence who controlled the trades. There were 7 major guilds, 5 middle, and 9 minor.

Armillary Sphere - These represent the heavens and stars around the Earth and Sun.

Apse - A semicircular area in the floor-plan of a church holding the high altar.

Baldachin - A canopy either attached the walls, suspended from the ceiling, or free standing with columns, over a sacred space.

Bas-Relief - A low-relief sculpture.

Baptistery - Building used for Christian baptisms; many times shaped in an octagon or circle.

Campanile - Italian for "bell tower." Usually they were tall enough for the citizens to hear the bells from a distance.

Canto - This has a few meanings. A canto is a section in a long poem or could be a song. Another meaning is corner.

Cappella - Chapel.

Caryatid - A supporting pillar in the form of a woman.

Cartouche - A design or emblem representing a family.

Cenquecento - A time period during the decline of the arts.

Cloister - An open space in a church or monastery surrounded by a columned or arched walkway.

Crenellation - Notches along the top of many fortified battlements, the open spaces were used for defense.

Cupola - A rounded vault or ceiling dome.

Crypt - Vaulted space usually underground that contained buried tombs.

Diptych - An altarpiece usually made of 2 equal panels hinged together.

Duomo – Means "Domas Dei," or "House of God" in Latin.

Epitaph - A tomb inscription containing a brief description of the deceased.

Façade - The front wall or face of a building.

Firenze - The name of the city of Florence in old Italian. The ancient name was Florentia.

Fleur-de-lis - *A representation of a lily or a Fiordalisa. This is a major symbol of the city of Florence.*

Florin - *In 1252 the guild of Arti de Cambio introduced this golden coin that would be used as currency in Europe until 1533.*

Fresco - *A form of painting using pigments painted directly into wet plaster. Also called "buon fresco."*

Gia - *On streets you may see the word "Gia" before the street name; this means "used to be."*

Gilding - *an application of thin leaf gold over a product.*

Gnomon - *An upright sundial that casts shadows onto the surface.*

Grotesques - *A style of art named by Raphael containing sphinxes, monsters, and other imaginary creatures.*

Humanism - *A period of time when people were studying the classics of Rome and Greece. This became the beginning of the Renaissance.*

Lantern - *A cylindrical structure located at the top of a dome usually containing windows for admitting light.*

Loggia - A covered, open-air gallery or arcade usually with braces or columns.

Lunette - A semicircular space above a door; it can be either plain or decorated.

Marzocco - A ferocious appearing lion holding a shield with a fleur-de-lis which is a symbol of Florence.

Nave - The central main aisle in a church; the congregation sits on either side.

Obelisk - A tall stone pillar with four sides and a pyramidal top.

Oculus - A round opening or window at the top of a dome to admit light. The eye of the building.

Oltrarno - The other side of the Arno River.

Opera - You will notice this word everywhere. It means by the official workshop or administrative office of a cathedral or palace.

Perspective - The art of creating something that appears three dimensional.

Piazza - An open city square.

Piagnoni - Followers of the Monk Savonarola, called the "Criers" or "The Weepers."

Glossary

Predella - Artwork, located at the bottom of an altarpiece or sculpture, related to the theme of the main artwork.

Priori - The ruling committees of Florence.

Putto - A plump, naked young male with wings, associated with Cupid or Eros, the god of love. The plural is Putti.

Quatrefoil - A lobed design with four sides used in Gothic art and architecture.

Refectory - The dining hall for nuns or monks in a convent or monastery.

Reliquary - An object in which holy relics are held.

Romanesque - 10th and 12th century European architecture style influenced by the Romans.

Rustication - Heavy, roughhewn stone blocks used in building.

Sarcophagus - A funeral monument usually a stone coffin elaborately decorated with carvings or paintings.

Tabernacle - Popular since the 12th century, these adorned houses, and mostly outdoor corners decorated with religious images for people to pray at. Also found inside churches as a canopied cover for an image.

Telamon - *A supporting pillar in the shape of male.*

Terra cotta - *Baked earth, usually unglazed red, used for roof tiles and bricks.*

Terribilita - *Something meant to show power and induce fear.*

Tondo and Roundels - *A circular painting or sculpture.*

Transept - *Two aisles located off the nave forming the shape of a cross.*

Trompe l'oeil - *A painting style meant to fool the eye; looks three-dimensional.*

Tympanum - *A triangular space above the façade of a building.*

Sources

Stones of Florence
Mary McCarthy
1963 Edition
A Harvest Book   Harcourt Inc., NY
15 E. 6th St., NY, NY 10010

Florence - The Biography of a City
Christopher Hibbert
1st American edition 1993
W.W. Norton and Comp Inc.
500 5th. Ave., NY, NY

The Renaissance - A Short History
Paul John 2000
A Modern Library Chronicles Book
Random House

Santa Maria Novella
Copyright 2000
Editrice Giust di Becocci Saverio s.t.l.
Largo Liverani 12/3 504141 Firenze, Italy

The Rise and Fall of the House of Medici
Christopher Hibbert
Penguin Books 1974

Piazza del Duomo
Rev. Timothy Verdon
Diocesan office for Catechesis through Art

Horizon - A Magazine of the Arts
Spring, Volume X, Number 2, 1968
American Heritage Publishing Company Inc., U.S.A.

So, you are going to Italy and if I were going with you these are the things I would invite you to do.
Clara E. Laughlin
Houghton Mifflin Co.
Riverside Press - Cambridge, MA 1925

San Miniato al Monte
Lica Bertani & Becocci Editore
Presentation by Bruno Santi
Copyright 2010 ATS Italia Editrice
Via di Brava 41/43 00163 Roma
Largo Liverani 12/13- 50141 Firenze, Italy

National Geographic
Volume 132 No.1 July 1967
National Geographic Society
Washington, DC

Handbook to Life in Renaissance Europe
Sandra Sider
Facts on file 2005

Florence and Tuscany - Eyewitness Travel Guide
Dorling Kindersley, London, England 1995

Secret Florence
Niccolo Rinaldi
Jonglez 2012

Sources

Brunelleschi's Dome
Ross King Co. 2000
Penguin Group
Penguin, Putman, Inc. 375 Hudson St., NY, NY 10014

The Handy Art History Answer Book
Madelyn Dickerson 2013
Visible Ink Press Detroit, MI

The Great Masters
Giorgio Vasari, translation by Gaston Du C de Vera
Beaux Arts Editions
1986 Hugh Lauter Associates, Inc.

The Ugly Renaissance
Alexander Lee 2013
Double Day NY, NY

Florence
Frances King
Newsweek Book Edition 1982

Italy - Out of Hand. A Capricious Tour
Barbara Hodgson Co. 2005
Chronicle Books LLC   85 2nd St., San Franciso, CA 94105

Florence, A Delicate Case
David Leavitt 2002
Bloombury, New York, and London

Florence Art and Architecture
Various Authors 2005
Magnus Edizioni, Udine Italy
Assoc. Cambridge Publishing

Art History - Revised Edition 1
Marilyn Stokstad in collaboration with Bradford Collins 1999
Prentice Hall, Inc., and Harry Abrams Publishing

Art History - 2nd Edition Volume 2
Marilyn Stokstad
University of Kansas
Prentice Hall Inc., and Harry Abrams Publishing

Santa Maria Novella
Aldo Tarquini O.P.
Becocci Editore

The Medici, Michelangelo and the Art of Late Renaissance Florence
In conduction with the exhibit at the Art Institute of Chicago
Yale University Press

Spoke and Emailed
Professor L. Fabbri @ opera duomo firenze

The Uffizi Gallery Tour
Bonechi Edizioni "Il. Turismo's" S.R.I.
Via dei Rustici, 5 Florence, Italy

Santa Maria Novella
www.museicivicflorentini.it/SMM

Strolling though Florence
Franco Ciarleglio
Florence, Italy 2003

Florence web guide: Your insiders guide to Florence, Italy
www.florencewebguide.com

The Basilica of Santa Croce
Itinerary guide 2003 Opera di Santa Croce sillabe
S.R.I. Livorno
www.sillabe.it

www.ingramcontent.com/pod-product-compliance
Lightning Source LLC
Chambersburg PA
CBHW040201100526
44592CB00001B/2